The Controlled Demolition of White America

Ashley Morgan

Ashley Morgan

Copyright © 2011 Ashley Morgan

Cheers Production

Baltimore, MD

ISBN: 1461085071
ISBN-13: 978-1461085072

LCCN: 2011928034

DEDICATION

I dedicate this book to my father who always sent me on the
right path in life.

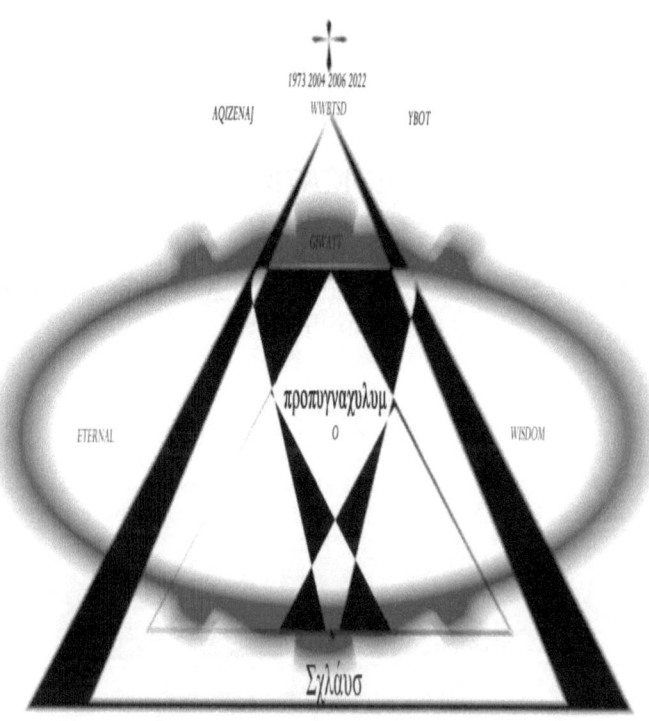

CONTENTS

INTRODUCTION

Throughout the history of the United States, Christianity has always been a major player. In fact, this country was founded upon the religion of Christianity. We learn in schools that Christianity is a "White" religion, but for those of us who read the Bible know that Adam and Eve were created in the Garden of Eden over near Ethiopia in Africa. This means that Adam and Eve were probably Black, or at least we can say they were not White with a high degree of certainty. But the thing is that it really doesn't matter because God created us *all* and in His image. We all represent Him and we are all one people with the same roots. God does not separate us out and say "Oh, you are this color – so you are of less value." No! God loves us all with equal love. It is man with his jealousy, boastfulness, pride, and arrogance that he tries to set himself apart from other men in effort to make himself appear like he is a god in the eyes of other men. This "better than you" attitude has no color preference. It will devour anyone who will host its addictive oblivion. In the past, White and Black separation had enveloped the nation as a whole, even though the country was built as a result of the two races teaming up from the beginning. But over time, Whites began to be portrayed as horrible people who were somehow "above" Blacks on the importance scale. Today, the idea that Whites are above Blacks is quickly reversing to the polar opposite.

What a nice world we live in… a place where White people have no place in society anymore. What a nice world we live in… a place where you get more rights and benefits if you are anything but White. What a nice world we live in… a place where White people have worked to support all the other races for decades and now are being edged out of the job market. What a nice world we live in where Whites have fought for centuries to make everyone equal, but are now victims and trodden under foot by every race including other Whites. What a nice world we live in where White youth of today no longer know how to act as a White person. What a nice world we live in where Whites wear their pants hanging down to their knees and talking "G" in their plight to be accepted by Blacks so they can move up a notch (in their minds) in society. What a lovely world we live in where this book will probably be antagonized as being a "racist" book because it was written by a White person. Welcome to a new world. Welcome to a world where Whites are quickly becoming the minority and being treated as cattle where their thoughts no longer count (unless they are among the few Whites that still have money). Welcome to a changing world in which if you are White, you may not like what tomorrow may bring for you. Welcome to the controlled demolition of White America.

CHAPTER 01: THE DISCOVERY

According to the history that many of us were taught in school, Whites and Blacks have always been separated. America always belonged to White people and Blacks were always the slaves. Foreigners and other races were not discussed much except for the idea that they do not belong in America, even though some managed to "slip through the cracks". Many people still live and die to this reality that they have been taught, however, I suggest that you open your eyes to the actual reality. In other words, try and erase your mind of these wrong ideas and reboot your thoughts by observing everything going on around you with new eyes. I suggest the reality that many of us hold is wrong and it has been placed in our thoughts on purpose by various people throughout our lives and from history books. Many of the people who originated these thoughts had an agenda – to destroy White "supremacy" and to raise up Blacks and other races. While other people responsible for these ideas were not aware of an agenda, but just rode the coat tails of the people with this agenda and helped to spread the seeds of their ideas. The ideas I will discuss with you are obvious once you begin to focus in on them and you can begin to reverse all the things you have been taught that are wrong.

But it will definitely take some effort and cooperation on your part. You have to remove the prejudice that you hold inside yourself. You have to realize this hate has been taught to you and that you have this hate for no real reason. If you can work with me and put this all away, read on. If not, go ahead and close this book right now because you will not benefit from it until you are ready for it.

I analyze Blacks compared to Whites throughout this book. I am not prejudice and have no hate for Blacks. I love all people of all races, but at times I may touch a nerve here or there and that is because you still have a lot of wrong ideas to work out of your own mind. I use the term "White(s)" for Caucasians or White people and "Black(s)" to refer to people you may think of as African Americans. Just ride with me to the end and I would love to hear your comments. Write me a short email at this address ashleymorgan@usa.com .

We will start off by analyzing our wrong thoughts. We can begin with the history of Whites and Blacks in the United States and think it through together. Let's start off from the "beginning" times when America was first being populated and civilized by foreigners. You were always taught that America was "discovered". This is a lie and you will know this if you just think about it for a moment. Erase from your mind this lie that you have been taught, and think about it. We know that "Native Americans" were always here before we took over. So to get to the truth we have to erase the lie that America was discovered and realize the truth that people already lived here and were killed almost completely out of existence by foreigners – our ancestors. Our ancestors were quickly using up all the resources in their own country due to modernization and they needed new lands to "rape" their resources from. They took ships and sailed to what we now label as America and killed nearly all the people who lived there and took away not only their land, but their very existence and culture.

So, who were these ancestors that came to America and killed all the inhabitants? They were people from England, Spain, France, and all over the modernized world. They were accompanied by people from many parts of Africa (brought here as slaves). They first fought to kill the inhabitants that lived here, and then fought each other to control the resources.

The first inhabitants sent here to live were criminals and poor people whom the countries sent here, partly because they wanted them removed from their society. They were also sent here to tame the land and make it easier to navigate and survive in. Basically, these criminals paved the way to make everything *safer* for others to come here after them. It was probably a good deal in some ways for the criminals too because they obtained freedom, but they had to survive in harsh lands, so there was definitely a tradeoff.

For the poor that were sent, it was a means for them to make their own in a land that did not cost them any money. They could cut trees down and build a home for themselves and their families. They would also get the claim to the land around their house as their own. This was a pretty good deal for the poor who didn't mind a little hard work.

It was a well orchestrated plan. Notice that America was "discovered" in 1492, but it was almost 300 years before the country would be labeled as an actual country in 1776. Why did it take so long? Well, it takes time to kill all the residents of a country and then tame the land to make it livable for wealthy people. Only then, could it be a place with some kind of basic organization in which it could be controlled by the wealthy. If the land was still nothing but wild forests with lots of wild animals, diseases, and dangers, then there still would be no Declaration of Independence or established government of any kind.

With all that being said, part of the taming process included sending people to America that were less in the eyes of society – people whom it would not matter if they lived or died. This would be a long process and they knew this. Therefore, to speed things up, part of the plan included "purchasing" people to do the deeds and works of these wealthy people's bidding. This meant they made trips to the huge continent of Africa – where Black people lived whom were totally uneducated, totally unethical, and totally ungodly – and used them to work alongside the criminals and poor.

Slavery was an invention of the African people. There were Africans who used their own people as slaves to do work in Africa. It was a common practice all over the modern world at that time to purchase these slaves from their African owners to do work that wealthy people did not want to do. Since the African owner could simply go capture more slaves for free, they gladly sold their slaves.

The Africans were so immoral that they sold their own people for things such as snail shells! Look it up. Slaves were purchased with cowry shells. Can you imagine the horrors these "slaves" were sold into simply for a shell? Here is a link if you want to see more information on this: http://en.wikipedia.org/wiki/African_slave_trade

Once these people were bought, they were taken by ships to the Americas and the Caribbean islands to inhabit them and do the work they were directed to do. The ethical thing for these countries to have done would have been to stop Africans from using their people as slaves. Instead, they just looked around to see if anyone was watching and then bought some people from the Africans and used them for their own deeds. It's kind of like drug dealers on the street where unethical police see a drug deal going down between a couple of youth and then they go bust them. However, instead of arresting them, they let them go but take the drugs for their own use.

The Africans actually probably had training courses for a few extra shells. "If he acts out, jus lash m wit za whip!" The White guy was like "Really? Are you sure? Just la…" (African interrupts) "Here lez me show you sir. Jus lash…" "White guy interrupts… "*OK, OK* I think I got it!" Seriously though, not to make light of it, but it was very common practice in those days and times and no one really even thought anything about slavery. We are actually quickly returning to those days and you may see slavery return in your lifetime so prepare yourself. But we will discuss this later.

The slaves, criminals, and poor people would do all the physical work of cleaning the country up to make it livable (cutting trees, shrubs, and making roads), planting fields for a constant supply of food, and helping to kill the natives who were already living here.

The farming was so good that it eventually developed into business – meaning that the goods being made and the crops being grown were sold and sent over to Europe and other places. The land here was very rich in nutrients and produced bigger and better tasting crops. The timber was really tall and bigger around because it was literally untouched to that point in time.

This began to attract wealthy business men to the idea of profit. They hired men whom they sent over to America to manage their business of farming and cropping. They became so profitable that they created more farms and therefore, their demand for slaves went up. There were Whites who worked as slaves, but they were called "indentured servants" instead of "slaves". The difference was the indentured servant was not owned. They did not get paid wages either but worked for food and a place to live just like the slaves did. They worked on contracts of usually 3 to 7 year time periods.

There were also wealthy Black men who were slave owners and ran their own farms, even though you don't hear about them much. This fact has been stamped out by the people with the agenda. In fact, Blacks have always been very similar to Whites. There have always been wealthy Black people, educated Black people, and even much of our inventions and technology today is the result of Black people throughout history that have worked and put forth their part in society just like Whites. However, again, these facts have been suppressed over time in order to continue the agenda. I will be referring to this agenda many times throughout this book so when I do refer to it from now on, I will simply call it "The Agenda". This will be our code word to sum the entire idea up in just two words.

The reality of slavery was bad in some instances, but was not nearly as bad in general as most people believe. One bad instance of the reality were that slaves were brought to North America, South and Central America, Caribbean Islands and other places around the world in bad conditions – crowded boats and were treated like cattle and then brought to their final destination to be sold for a profit.

However, this is how travel on ships were in general during these times. If you can remember, the people who sailed over on the Mayflower traveled in similar conditions. This is because technology did not advance until centuries later to make travel healthier and more enjoyable. All people who traveled by ship on the ocean in these days did it knowing they were risking their life.

The whole process of getting slaves from Africa to America was designed like a production line. The first men paid were the Africans who sold their own people for profit – I suppose money *is* the root of all evil.

The second men paid were the men (whether White or Black) who bought the slaves and transported them to America (or whatever destination) and auctioned them off for a profit to the farm owners (who also came to be known as slave owners).

Finally, the slaves were taken to their destination which was the farm where they would live and work. Many slave owners were nice while others were very mean. However, we always hear about the worst stories – just like everything else in the world. People thrive on negativity for some reason. The slaves would sometimes get sold around among slave owners so slaves were not guaranteed a permanent address.

Slaves were workers. For their work they received food, shelter, and some clothing and household items including things like blankets and everyday needs. Some farmers would give them all they needed plus more while others purposely skimped and didn't supply enough (obviously this was the bad owners). If you wanted a comparison of a bad slave owner in today's world it would be companies and organizations that refuse to give their employees a retirement and/or they pay them as low wages as possible. This is about 90% of employers today. Instead of giving you a retirement – they make you pay for it yourself through a 401K savings plan.

The slaves worked long hard days from sunup to sundown (as everyone in those days did). For some of them who were new to slavery, this was a big change from their days in Africa where they were running around naked and not having to do much during the day. There were a certain few who were hunters in Africa because someone had to get the food, but that just consisted of spearing an animal and then eating it. The position as a slave in America was very hard because they had people over them all day telling them what to do and making sure they worked all day every day. It definitely was very hard, hot and sweaty work that most people in America today would not be able to handle.

This is where the concept of factory work was developed. In factories, there are managers that make people work in lines creating their products that they sell for profit. The managers work for the owner and owners are rarely seen by the employees. The employees are given barely enough money to buy or rent their own place to live, food, and clothing. Instead of beating the workers, managers just threaten to fire them – essentially taking away their life (can't buy food, can't buy clothing, and can't buy shelter). Slavery never died. It is still alive and well today. It just works slightly different and everything has different labels (for example: a slave is now called an employee, etc.).

Slavery was also worldwide, not just in the United States. In fact, slavery continued in South America for some time after slavery was made illegal in the United States. After slavery was made illegal, there were many slaves that did not want it to end because this was like their job – their livelihood. Today, this would be like creating a law that having an employee is illegal. Many slaves chose to stay with their slave masters after slavery ended and work as an "employee".

Now, over time, technology improved and there was a move among wealthy people to become even more wealthy. They wanted to have less people work for them and yet get more money. They had to have a plan – The Agenda. Making slavery illegal was the first step in this process. This allowed them to continue what they were doing (having others do their hard work for them) but without having a responsibility for the person. In other words, if someone owned a slave – that was an investment. They had to keep the slave happy and healthy to a certain extent to get the work out of them. If the slave died or ran away, (or just got too old to work) they lost money. Owners did not like this. As time passed and slaves grew tired and weary of doing all this work, they became more restless and more unruly, causing the owners to really consider a new technique.

The idea of outlawing slavery was the perfect answer for the rich man. They could just call everyone an "employee" and pay them really, really low wages – just enough to feed them and keep them alive and well enough to work. If the "employee gave them problems, they simply fired them with absolutely no financial or legal responsibility to them at all. This was a huge change from the past, where they were liable legally for anything their slave did for their entire life. If a slave went down the road to a farm and destroyed crops, then the owner was responsible – because the slave was considered to be their "property". With the idea of calling the slave an "employee" and making them no longer be considered their "property", business men were now able to treat their slaves worse by firing them and leaving them at the mercy of the wilderness with absolutely no responsibility for their life thereafter and no financial loss at all. This new idea of considering a slave an employee was terrific for the owners!

However, there were some people who did not like this idea. They wanted things to stay the same. These were usually the owners who treated their slaves good and were getting plenty of work out of slaves with very little hassle. These owners wanted to take care of their slaves because it was a beneficial arrangement for both the slave and slave owner. The slaves were treated well and given things they needed. In return, the owner got plenty of good work done by happier, healthier slaves.

The bad owners had mistreated their slaves. They did not care about their slaves, but instead cared about getting more money and power, and/or meeting their demands and timelines of the owners (sometimes the managers of the farms were just managers hired by the owners who lived overseas). They had lost money on slaves due to them not doing good quality work, running away, or destroying property in which they were held financially liable for. When slaves did bad things, owners had to decide whether to beat them in effort to teach them a lesson or just kill them and lose all the money invested in that slave. The slaves were rebellious because of the fact they were being treated bad so it became a vicious cycle where the owner/manager could not manage the farm and it was not as profitable as it once was. So the idea of an employee/employer relationship seemed like a better idea for these bad owners.

This eventually led to the Civil War – a battle of ideas on the future of how business would be ran and how wealth would be distributed. I know, you were taught that this was a war to end slavery and give Blacks their rights. That is slightly true, but now you can see the reality of what was really going on. It was a battle over which way was a better method of making money: enslavement or employment.

When slavery was ended and the employment idea started to take form, the world had to change and adapt. If you notice, it was not just America that outlawed slavery, it was a worldwide decision. All the modernized countries outlawed slavery and adapted this new and improved "employment" system. This new system was also "color blind" so that the indentured servants would have a place in the new system as well. In fact, part of The Agenda was to make anyone and everyone an employee and this is the system we still have in place today.

The Agenda was created by some very elect individuals to create a perfect plan for them and their descendants to rule over the entire world – not just a farm. From their experiences with slavery they saw that people who were kept in constant fear and were not given any financial authority could very easily be controlled. If you control someone's food, then you control their life! The fact to prove this is in the idea that slaves could have taken over if they really wanted to. Slaves worked physically hard. That means they were very strong. Also, slaves outnumbered the owners by great numbers. It should have been a no brainer for the slaves to have simply killed the owners and managers of the farms and just taken control. That did not happen. Why? Because slaves were in constant fear and they were kept depressed and at the lowest point mentally and financially as possible.

In other words, slaves were just making it paycheck to paycheck and they did not want to mess that up because they were always thinking it could be worse. They just wanted things to keep going as is – yeah it wasn't much, but it was better than nothing and was certainly better than taking such a big risk by trying to take over. Every slave would have to have been on the same page, but you know how humans are. There were probably smart ones who talked about the idea and when a few others started to get on board there was someone who started talking negative and telling them that they would not be able to do it...

(Grandma) "Johnny you just shut your mouth boy and stop talking nonsense! You're going to get us all killed up in here. Now get over there and check the winda (window) and make sure the owner isn't outside a listening!"

In the end, slavery just had to play out until finally there was enough onboard that they really would have succeeded and that is why the wealthy had to come up with a different plan before all Hell broke loose.

So after slavery was an adjustment period. The wealthy had to give answers as to why they were switching things up. And they used the idea that slavery was a "bad" thing that had been "happening to" Blacks and they (the owners and the government) were here to make things all better. They pretended it was something they were doing to benefit Blacks, instead of the truth – that they were doing it to benefit themselves. This explanation calmed the Blacks down and outraged the Whites (poor Whites and good slave owners). There were so many slave owners that had treated their slaves good and in fact, there were thousands of poor Whites that had helped slaves to escape to freedom via an "underground railroad" – a network of White people who helped Blacks get from house to house, town to town, until they entered free territory. Then the Whites helped them to build their own homes and helped them get established in a new life.

But now, the government began to frame slavery in a light where Whites were evil bad people and Blacks were poor mistreated people – which was a complete lie in most cases and was true to only a handful of certain people, but not true for the majority at all. This is what began to cause a divide between Whites and Blacks. This is how the racial hate we see in America today began.

Things like the KKK and the Black Panthers eventually came into existence. There were times when Blacks and Whites began to hate each other so much that they did not want to mix at all. The slogan "separate but equal" came to the forefront of the media, hyping up the idea that Blacks and Whites could live and work in the same cities and towns but they did not have to mix anything. They had separate restrooms, water fountains, bus seats, dining areas, and the list goes on and on. However, even though they would be separate, they would remain unequal as far as legal rights. This idea obviously did not work and was eventually changed.

Why is everyone so against each other today? There is no real answer if you think about it – but most Blacks and Whites both will tell you it's because of the Whites enslaving the Blacks. Now no one today has ever been a slave and neither has their mother or father and most people's grandparents were not slaves, and even beyond that. This also means that no person alive today has ever been a slave owner. In fact, slavery began to be debated in the mid-to-late 1700's and ended in the 1800's. Today is nearly 200 years later and we are still acting like it happened yesterday. Why? Has anyone ever stopped to ask why? There can be a major earthquake where thousands are killed and we forget all about it in a couple of days because it is "old news". Yet slavery that ended over 200 years ago gets people more upset and angry today than it did back then. Why?

This is another part of the bigger governmental plan to control people and take away their freedom of choice and power – The Agenda. To make The Agenda work, they must first keep people in fear (911 and Wars on Terror, racial hate, etc.) and secondly, they must not be obligated in any way for the life and health of people that create their wealth. They must be able to get rid of these workers at the snap of a finger with no obligation, not even a retirement package or social security. Thirdly, they must keep the workers in such poverty that workers can see no way out, nor must they develop a desire to get out in fear of messing up the little amount they do have. This way, the poor workers will actually help them to maintain their system. This system is the system we live in today. The wealth is all getting taken by the very top wealthy people and they are getting exponentially wealthier and more powerful as the years tick by. It's like sucking the ice cream out of a cup through a straw. The middle class has been almost completely dissolved, and you are supposed to feel "lucky" if you even have a job today.

America is long overdue for rebellion by the citizens and the government and wealthy know this. That is why they want us as a people to be separated on ideas because if we were to ever get on the same page again, we might just take over! We are in exactly the same place that the slaves were, except worse because they were guaranteed to be taken care of because they were owned whereas we are at the mercy of the streets if we don't obey them and keep The Agenda going! In the next few chapters, I will discuss the ideas that got us here and why it continues to work.

CHAPTER 02: THE DIVISION

There were many Whites in the "New World" and they were able to gain wealth. There were also many Blacks achieving wealth as slave owners, but fewer in number. All was well for everyone until the split on methodology for wealth creation began – slavery vs. employee methods. Again, what caused this separation was the fact that good slave owners began to outdo the bad slave owners financially. This happened because the slaves of the bad owners were rebelling in various ways and on multiple levels – resulting in less production (not meeting deadlines, shipment amounts, etc.) So bad slave owners were the ones pushing for the abolishment of slavery because they were upset that they were losing money. The good slave owners were not for the idea of ending slavery, because for the most part everyone, including their slaves, had a pretty fair situation and were somewhat content and happy with the way things were.

The slaves of the good owners had a much better life in America than they had in Africa (although they may have gone through a lot on their journey to that farm). They were actually better taken care of. Even the slaves of bad slave owners were somewhat better off. They were beaten when they did not get along with the owners or they rebelled – so those particular slaves had it worse. Although they were always at the threat of punishment, they were better off than they were in Africa where it was a wild jungle or barren dessert depending on which part of Africa they came from. This is why slaves never returned to Africa. Even after slavery was made illegal, they chose to stay right here in America, some remaining with their owners until death by their own choice.

Money has always been the root of all evil and there have always been battles for wealth but never to the extent of today. Ever since the division of ideas formed (slavery versus employee), there has been a vicious battle for wealth unlike any that ever existed in all of history. The race for wealth goes beyond healthy business competition. The desire to outdo others financially is now done by rewriting history, using media to brainwash the public to adapt whatever beliefs the business wishes to impose upon them, and training children from birth to become a loyal customer for their lifetime (McDonalds and other businesses like this are obvious ones – e.g. "Happy Meals" and other children's marketing).

An example of businesses playing dangerous media games like this is around the time Obama first took office. The major car companies claimed to have mismanaged money and were now going to have to go out of business. They begged tax payers for a helping hand of not thousands, not millions, but *billions* of dollars to keep them afloat. In America, the idea has always been that if you don't manage your business finances properly, then you must go out of business.

If the government helps keep you in business, then you must live in a *communist* nation like Russia. Modern America has always been a *capitalist* nation – meaning that only the strong and fittest survive. You must be competitive in order to remain a player in the business world. If not, you have to go out of business. However, this all changed and America became a communist nation when we decided that big businesses were "too large to fail" and gave billions of dollars to them so they could keep people working and stay in business.

As if becoming a communist nation wasn't bad enough, the companies took the tax payer money and instead of using it to keep people employed, they used it to send their top executives on expensive vacations and bought personal aircraft for them. They went ahead and fired employees, had layoffs and the economy went down the drain in a hurry as a result. They had lied! These people should have been tarred and feathered for such treason! Instead they were rewarded.

As a result of all this, American citizens took their own action and began to stop purchasing their vehicles. Americans began to buy Toyota cars instead. Toyota's sales exploded and they became the number one seller of vehicles.

The angry American car companies decided to take hurtful action against Toyota by telling lies about the company (trying to destroy Toyota). They hired people to claim that Toyota had a gas pedal that would stick and cause you to wreck and die. They flooded the media with pictures of cars that had crashed and caught on fire – wreaking havoc and terror on the minds of citizens. Did you hear me? When they wrecked, it didn't just crash, but it also burned completely up! How dumb do you have to be to believe that nonsense? A gas pedal sticks and the driver never had sense enough to put on their brake? Regardless, American citizens began to develop fear toward purchasing Toyota cars. Several years later in 2011, it was revealed that there was never a problem with the Toyota cars at all. The story telling the truth was a very subtle, small story in the news that not many people heard. The companies did their evil deed of placing fear into people and succeeded in getting them to continue giving their money to American car manufacturers while Toyota suffered for no reason.

This is just one simple example of how media is used to control the populations of people today. It is the same technique they used in slavery and it is the same technique they use today. Their technique is to keep people in confusion and fear and then tell them the solution is to give them your money and everything will be ok. 911 is just another example on a much larger scale.

So how did this play out when it came to Whites and Blacks after the abolishment of slavery? It all started before the Civil War. They began creating campaigns to control people's thoughts. The following are some actual examples from various times:

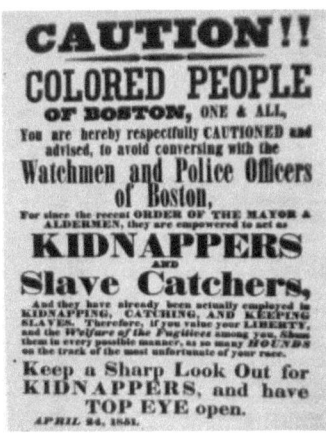

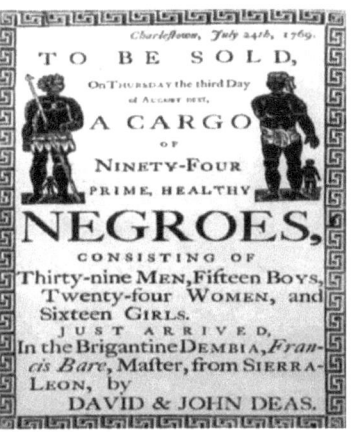

100 DOLLARS
REWARD!

Ranaway from the subscriber on the 27th of July, my Black Woman, named

EMILY,

Seventeen years of age, well grown, black color, has a whining voice. She took with her one dark calico and one blue and white dress, a red corded gingham bonnet; a white striped shawl and slippers. I will pay the above reward if taken near the Ohio river on the Kentucky side, or **THREE HUNDRED DOLLARS**, if taken in the State of Ohio, and delivered to me near Lewisburg, Mason County, Ky.   **THO'S. H. WILLIAMS.**
August 4, 1853.

There have been so many advertisements of ideas of which people willingly accept as true

that it all becomes part of people's daily reality.

I stopped watching television altogether because I started to realize how much of my life memories and ideas were false. These lies were taught to me over time by means of television and other media. Here is an experiment I dare you to try. That's right! I said *dare*. So are you up for it? I dare you to stop watching television altogether. Stop watching movies. Stop reading the newspaper. Stop going online and reading things. I bet you will not be able to do it. That is because the government has taught you that you cannot live without it. It was very difficult for me to stop at first.

If you do try this and you tell others, you will find that they will try and talk you out of it. They will be against you. They will think you are weird. They will want to turn you in to some authority, but there is no law that says you *must* watch television (yet). So instead they will try to brainwash you into returning to media by giving you reasons to do it. One of the first reasons they will give you is this: "well, you really should watch because you need to be updated and know what is going on in the world."

In case you have never thought about it (and I am sure you haven't because you are kept from thinking for yourself in most cases) think about what you see on the news. Are you *really* affected by it? Have you ever seen the things on the news in your real life (besides others just verbally repeating the story to you)? I am willing to bet that you haven't. Oh sure there are some things that do happen in life, but does it really affect you?

Here are the things that I experienced just by cutting television and news out of my life (I also have not listened to music much at all). The first thing I noticed was emptiness. What do I do? What do I think? I was so used to some television or news report telling me what to do, what to think, and what my reality should be, that I had almost lost the ability to observe my surroundings for myself. I could look outside and see the weather for myself, but I did not trust me. Instead, I needed a weather man to tell me what my local weather was – even if he was wrong! What in the world is wrong with society? This is not just me, but it is *you* and everyone else you know too! If you don't believe me, then take on my challenge and just block all outside sources of information and just live your day to day life based on your own observations alone. You will see. It took me about 3 months to get past the initial sense of loneliness and emptiness I felt as a result of not watching television, but now I don't miss it at all. I laugh inside myself when I see everyone else so emotionally involved in the latest television show or whatever is going on in the news (everyone just so tied up in wondering who will get kicked off American Idol for instance). These things are totally irrelevant to life. Sometimes I do get curious about certain news stories, like the latest earthquake, but I hear enough about stories like that from others to get a sense of what happened without having to tune back in to media sources.

The first thing that happened when I stopped the media flow was initial emptiness. The second thing I noticed when I stopped the media flow into my head was that people around me tried to get me to continue the media flow. They did not like the fact that I was not participating in the media brainwashing game at all. They desperately wanted me to get back into it immediately. However, I continue to be media free for the most part. I listen to radio news maybe once every 3-4 months for just a few minutes (PBS radio). I still have people from time to time try and battle me into "watching television or else", but I just ignore their attempts and go on with my mostly media free-life while they sit there miserable because they want everyone else to be doing it too. I think this is a thing deep inside of them whereas they know that watching TV and other media is hurting them, but they also don't want to stop – it's an addiction. Addicts like to keep other people around them addicts as well so they don't feel as bad. Misery loves company, I guess is the saying that applies here.

The third thing I noticed was an improvement in my health both physically and mentally. I used to always be tense and nervous and on edge. I never realized it though. It was after several months of not having any media going into my system that one day I turned on the radio news and began listening to the daily events. I instantly noticed my heart beating faster in my chest and it actually began to pound. I was surprised at first and it really stood out to my awareness that my heart had sped up so dramatically. I almost couldn't believe it. I thought, "Did the media always do this to me?" The answer is *yes*, the media had always been doing this to me but I was so used to it that it was "normal". Not only did my heart speed up but I was more anxious feeling and I started becoming short on breath. I turned it off. I knew from that point forward I wanted to continue limiting what was going into my own thoughts. I want to control me.

I do not want someone or something else controlling me. I did not like it.

The forth thing I noticed was that I wanted to begin enjoying life more. What I mean is I wanted to get out and enjoy nature and the outdoors to experience life. I realized that my memories *were* my life. I thought back through the years of what I call my life. All I could remember was TV shows, movies, and commercials. There were some experiences I had with family and friends but very little in comparison to media.

I defined my own life and childhood like this:

• I thought I had family members somewhere out there named Willis and Arnold.
• I thought that my brother Marty was somewhere in another time and that is the reason why I hadn't seen him lately. Maybe he was with Doc.

• I sometimes wonder how George and Weezie are doing and if their dry cleaning business is still moving them on up.

I had to just stop and think for a minute. These people are not even real! They are so implanted in my memory as real people that I cannot change that part of my brain. I don't think I will ever be able to do that. I have been brainwashed. I have been made to believe a lie. If I actually had accurate memories of my life, I would see myself sitting in front of an electronic box called a television wasting my childhood away staring.

I now want to create my own memories that are real. I want to go fishing, hiking, swimming, walk on the beach, spend moments like this with family and friends in real life and not by texting them or talking on the telephone. I want a life that is real and I want to breathe clean fresh air into my lungs rather than sitting in front of a dusty computer or electronic flat screen television. Since I have started living this way, I notice I have more enjoyable memories and I feel healthier. Also my memories are real. The people I enjoyed activities with are real and I can connect with them and talk about the good times we had together.

If I called up Willis, he would not remember me because we have never met. He would want me to call him Todd... not Willis because his name is Todd. All of the memories of him on Different Strokes going through all the various situations he went through were made up stories. I remember them as though they were real though.

His (Todd Bridges) memories of the exact same shows would be totally different. His memories would be of producers, cameras and lights among other random things that he saw on the studio set. He knows the show was a totally made up act and therefore he never experienced the stories the way we did. We emotionally connected to the show and the characters, whereas he just connected with the people as fellow actors and actresses and the contents of the shows really had no effects at all on him except as becoming a memory of a job he once did as a child.

I said all of that to show you how much we are controlled by media. This has been happening for a very long time. The idea of "White supremacy" was *invented* to make Blacks angry and upset at Whites in general and to make Whites begin to hate Blacks. Why would a government want people to hate each other and always be in hate and distrust against one another? Why would a government propagate so many ideas like this and allow them to go on? Many people would say it is freedom of speech. But I would have you think about the reality. The government can and will stop freedom of speech if they do not want it to be expressed.

There are many examples of this, but the one I will use is the example of the Christian God. The government has effectively shut down God inside the school walls altogether. If you even say the word "Jesus" inside a school, you are looking at possible expulsion as a student and a certain loss of your job as a teacher. However, you are looked down upon if you don't discuss Martin Luther King, the Black Panthers ideology, Muslims, Jews, or any other religion in the school setting. The only religion that people absolutely do not want to hear about is the Christian religion. Why? What is it that Christians believe that is so horrible? Well, they believe that it is wrong to kill, lie, cheat, steal, dishonor parents, live an immoral lifestyle, get divorced, be gay or lesbian, and finally they believe that Jesus Christ will save them and one day set them free from the mental slavery they lie victim to here on Earth today. All of these ideas are taboo in today's world. These are ideas that people today love and live by. Therefore, Christians are stepping on their toes. Christians make people feel guilty about living the way they live. That is why the Christian idea has been pushed out of society.

The process of removing Christianity from society was a process that was administered over a long time period though. It took over a hundred years for the people of the United States to evolve into the society it has become today.

Change is a process that happens in confusion, through a process of time, and through generations of peoples. How can confusion be created? Well, very simple. 911 and the ongoing War on Terror are how people of today are kept in confusion. There is literally a generation of people right now who are becoming teenagers that know only war. We have been in war their entire memorable life. That has shaped who these young people are in their personalities. They will always want to be in war, because they think it is just the normal way to be. This concept spreads throughout all aspects of their life too. They not only want to always be attacking other nations, but they attack friends and family verbally and think it is just normal to do this. They don't know life without conflict. They never have. They don't know life without fear. They never have. So how can you ever expect this generation to live by something they have never experienced – peace and security and love, for example? This generation has never experienced peace, security, or love and then we wonder why these kids will murder their best friend just for their tennis shoes.

The generation of the 1950's and 1960's were programmed heavily on the idea of White supremacy – a made up idea that Whites are more powerful and Blacks are nothing. This is false. Whites are not better and there have always been wealthy and powerful Blacks. In fact, as a simple example, there are many Black inventors throughout history that were well educated. There have been Black leaders in all realms of life – from being leaders in the nation's army and security, to artists and actors, to biological and science discoveries, to doctors and medical workers, to every imaginable career we have ever had. So why do you believe that Blacks were always illiterate people who were dumb and pushed down in society by those evil White supremacy people?

Doesn't this sound similar to those bad "Muslim evildoers" remarks from Bushes Presidency? The fact is, all of this type of propaganda is fake and created by the government and the wealthy people of the nation to keep the majority of people in fear, in confusion, and not trusting one another, so that the government and these wealthy folks can go on with The Agenda of being the one source of power on Earth, a one world government, sort of the "god" of this entire world, if you will. The final plan will result in all people being slaves to a select few who will be all powerful and almighty. You will not have a choice, you will obey or die. That is the reality we will soon be facing. It is coming very quickly and the younger generations welcome it with open arms as long as they still get to text each other. For those of us that still have the power to think, get ready. It's coming.

The fact is that Blacks always had just as much opportunity, but when these ideas popped up in the media about White supremacy and similar ideas, people accepted them as truth and reality. They no longer thought for themselves.

In fact, a great example of this kind of brainwashing happened in 1939 when the story War of the Worlds broadcast on the radio. It was portrayed as a real news broadcast about aliens that had landed on earth and were attacking. This was done to put fear into people and it worked. According to newspapers of that time, there were people who actually committed suicide out of the extreme fear they had. Today, you will see reports that the newspapers fabricated the stories and that no one actually committed suicide. So which newspaper lied? …the newspapers of today or the newspapers of the time when it occurred? One of them is obviously lying and the other is not. It doesn't matter. Either they committed suicide or not, but the point is that the fear was put into the people through the use of media.

This story was actually a government experiment to see just how effective their brainwashing was as to that point in time. Would people completely rely on them for their thoughts or not? They had been working for years to get to this point. The answer was yes, the people did believe everything they said – hook line and sinker – just like today. Yes this *is* still very true today. However, most people of today probably would not commit suicide if they heard that aliens were attacking Earth.

However, people are in confusion. That is what wealthy people and the government want more than anything is the ability to confuse you. In the nineties, there was a generation getting older that thought they had it all together. They could think for themselves. They were taught from opposing media sources (anti-government rock bands like Metallica, Pink Floyd and other sources) to think freely and to not trust the government. Whenever, the government took notice that this generation was becoming adults and were beginning to affect things like laws and other people's thoughts, 911 was initiated as a counter attack to make everyone in society confused – wondering what is *really* going on here. What is it that is happening? Because their only thoughts they had to rely on were the thoughts from the media that had been programmed into them their whole life, they could not discover an answer of clarity.

There were some free thinkers that exposed the whole situation, showing proofs from the actual video footage that aired that day, but people still do not want to believe it was done with explosives inside the buildings. They are afraid to think that 911 was an inside job because they will feel even more insecure than they already are. It is confusing, it is frightening, and you don't know who to trust. This is exactly where they want you. Are you there? This is the state of mind they had people in the past generations, but instead of it being 911, it was "White supremacy" and "Black uprising". Blacks and Whites did not trust each other and were confused about each other and were afraid of each other. This confusing idea is still here and still propagated to this day. Why let your mind be victimized by this nonsense? Live a life where you control your own thoughts. Turn off the media flowing into your thought world and take control.

CHAPTER 03: THE DIFFERENCES

After the successful attacks on people's thoughts with the term "White supremacy", new terms were quickly introduced to fuel the fire. They wanted to fuel the fire because thoughts become actions. Now that these negative thoughts took root, people were reacting by taking action. This is where you saw the uprising of Black "heroes" like Martin Luther King Jr. and Jesse Jackson. These men were "heroes" because they talked and spouted things from their mouths that embodied the anger many Blacks felt as a result of the brainwashing that had occurred in their mentality. They felt a hate and resentment toward Whites and Whites revolted with a similar hate back toward Blacks causing another uprising of the *KKK*. Everyone hated each other for having whatever skin tone. Doesn't that sound really silly? I mean come on, hate someone with such a deep hatred because of their skin tone? These people were so brainwashed that they couldn't see straight and we are not out of the woods yet.

This racism demon will exist for a long time from now. Even though people are getting more educated, they continue trying to substantiate the hate through new avenues. This has happened for a many years. The initial reason for the hate was because Whites kept Blacks as slaves and beat and tortured them. Then the reason had to change as the next generation was not slaves. So the reason twisted into the idea that this generation was "discriminated against" after slavery was over. New laws came into effect to address their concerns. One of these laws was segregation. Segregation was basically saying, "Well, we all have to live and work in society but we cannot get along. Therefore, we will separate ourselves from each other as much as possible while using the same infrastructure to live and exist in, yet we will all be equal with each other." This appeared to be the solution to all problems. However, segregation did not work because there was more propaganda (news stories and media) to follow telling Blacks that they were actually jacked and got the short end of the stick.

Blacks were upset by this and wanted things to go back to how it was before – reintegration. So ever since then, society has been working to reintegrate everyone back together. This has happened so far institutionally, but not socially. Neighborhoods are still segregated for the most part. There are Black neighborhoods and White neighborhoods and very little mixed neighborhoods. Also, everyone is still split as to which idea is best, integration or segregation?

Since the days of segregation, the new words that have come into play have been "minority" and "African American", both of which are very derogatory terms. "Minority" sounds like someone who is less than, someone who does not mean as much or have as much value as others. "Minority" is used to describe mostly Blacks but has been transported across the board to mean anyone who is not White.

"African American" is a term used to describe all Blacks in the United States. This term makes it sound like the Black person is not of equal value with an American. They are African American – meaning that they are from Africa and just so happen to be in America. Most Black people do not have any problem with being referred to as African American – even though their family has been in America just as long, if not longer, than any of the Whites in America today. Their families came here and built much of the country before many of the Whites even came over. Yet they have no problem being referred to as "African American".

This will change one day, I am sure of it. Minority is also still widely used and no one even thinks anything of it. Blacks are happy to call themselves minorities and Whites are just as happy to refer to them that way. However, I think that if the real meaning comes out into the media, it will be a big issue that will cause another generation of hate toward each other. Keep your eyes open, it is likely to happen in the next few years. This is because the Black and White youths actually get along and like each other today. The people "in charge" don't like this and they have already put these words out there into society to "explode" them at just the right moment. The government works like that. They will help people get closer and act as if they are trying to help everyone to "just get along" and they are actually the culprits of everyone not getting along. Yes, they imposed these words into society years ago – I believe it was in the 1980's. Now it is about time for them to unleash the hidden meanings behind the words. They will put stories in the media to make it sound horrible and blame it on the Whites. They will say Whites created this terminology to put Blacks down and promote the White race. Just watch, its coming. Then they will come up with some new words to call Blacks. These new words will sound better at the time, but will have another negative connotation that they will "expose" years later again. It's kind of like the word "Negro". This was a term the government made up to describe Blacks instead of the word "nigger". Negro was a much more acceptable word and everyone was pacified. However, in time they revealed it to also be a "bad" word and now a Black person would be *very* offended if you called them a Negro. The government plays with people (on a large scale) like a scientist plays with a mouse in a maze. They are in complete control, while the mouse is confused and blindly wandering around trying to figure its surrounds out. As soon as the mouse figures the maze out, the scientist just switches it into a new maze, still the same game but a different maze. The mouse is now confused again.

To figure out the reality of life one needs to step back and get rid of all media influences. Try not looking at the magazine racks in stores as you stand in line to buy your food. Try not going onto the Internet or at least ignore the news postings that will pop up as you surf. Try not watching television and movies. Try not listening to the radio. Try not listening to music. Just get rid of all the noise in your life and I promise you that you will see a new you. You will also see how other people are influenced daily by the media they expose themselves to.

In fact, you should really protect your mind from all sources possible. Your mind is your most precious commodity. Your mind is who you are and you need to protect that with all your power. Whatever your mind thinks affects your entire health physically, mentally and especially spiritually. It does take a little time to get used to it but you will find yourself feeling better as time passes.

At first, you will find old memories popping up out of nowhere. (This is a result of your brain trying to clear out inconsistencies in your saved thoughts). You will have more intense dreams. You will start to feel younger and more energized. You will notice a big difference and so will everyone around you.

Another thing you should do is eat healthier. Get rid of all the soda and candy in your diet. Maybe a little real chocolate here or there would not hurt but stay away from all the colored candies (candy with dyes in them for coloring) and other junk that is out there. Much of our moods come from what we eat. Think about food like this: what tree did this grow on? If you cannot answer that, then it is probably not safe to eat. Think about a gummy worm. What tree did it grow from? None! It is actually made from sugar and pig hoofs! All gelatins are made from the hoofs of pigs. The hoofs are boiled and then the water gets real jelly-like. That clear jelly-like substance is called gelatin and is used in everything from jelly to gummy worms, to

Jell-O, to anything with that jelly-like texture. Sick huh?

Purchased meat is completely unhealthy. It is filled with hormones and chemicals that farmers are required by laws to put in the animals. These chemicals and hormones end up in you! Try drinking tea – tea that you boil yourself from tea bags. The bags are filled with tea leaves and this is about as natural as you make a drink besides just drinking water itself. Get bottled spring water. The water out of your faucet has so many chemicals it isn't funny. Don't believe me? Just go down to your local water treatment plant and ask a worker to give you a tour. Ask them to explain to you how the water is purified and made safe to drink. All the water, including your toilet when you flush it, goes to their plant and they just clean (or "treat") the water and send it back to your house as water again. That's why they call it a "water treatment plant". It is not healthy to drink.

Eat as close to raw vegetables as possible. Eat raw fruits and also exercise. Go to bed earlier and get as much sleep as you can get. You will start to find your life getting better.

The government wants people to always check with their doctor before making any changes in their life. I don't personally believe in this, but you do what you feel you got to do. The government has everyone believing they cannot make any kind of decisions in their life without a doctor telling them it's *OK*. Wow! A world where doctors are gods. Who would have ever guessed that doctors would have so much power today compared to just a hundred years ago? A curious thing that I am sure will crop up handy for the government someday soon. Maybe you will have to get a doctor's note to buy a new car? Who knows?

The idea with all these things is to keep us down, but not too down. Until they can get computers to be able to do all the work, they still need us slaves for a while. Therefore, keep on living, but just barely – at least that is the way they want it and that is the way it will remain. Want to feel better? Then go pay your local doctor. He will not fix your problems, but he will give you drugs that will make you *believe* you feel better.

Now that everyone is a slave – not just Blacks – it has become a world full of gloom and doom. There is no hope even left anymore and the government knows it. That is why Obama won the election. They had him run on promises of guess what... "Hope". But that is where it all ended. Hope is the wish for good things to come. However, when nothing good ever comes, all the hope is lost again.

So back to the idea of Black and Whites hating each other for no real reason... If you go to a playground and watch, you will see children playing together happily. I mean White children with Black children and with Asian children and on and on. They do not hate each other. In fact, they love each other. They enjoy hanging out with one another and playing together.

So what happens to people between childhood and adulthood? The answer is brainwashing and thought influence. About half of it comes from the media and the other half from "preprogrammed" adults teaching lies and wrong ideas to the children. If a Black adult sees a young Black person hanging out with a young White person, they will speak to that Black youth and tell them it is wrong. They will train them to hate. Why? Because there is something inherent in humans that make them desire to make their reality stay reality.

In other words, the adult could not fit the idea of Blacks and Whites hanging out together into their reality, so they had to brainwash the youth so the youth will think and process with the same wrong thoughts they received so that the youth comes to a very similar reality as them.

It's just like a computer virus. A virus is a bad file that will destroy the computer, yet the computer continues to spread the virus to other computers. Eventually, the youth will treat White people differently. The White will notice the different behavior from their Black friend and will stop hanging out as much – thinking the Black must not like them. Then the Black youth sees the White hold back and therefore begins to believe what the older Black told them is true and starts to develop hate toward White people. The White senses the hate and stops hanging out altogether. And now the circle of hate is complete and continues for another generation.

When will we ever stop? The answer is never. This is because you can erase a computer and start from scratch, but you cannot do that with the human mind. You have to work very hard to change old thoughts and thought patterns.

Protect your mind. Protect your health. Treat others well, even if they do not treat you well. It is a good idea to read the Bible daily to feed your mind with the truth. The Bible is the one and only source of truth and freedom in this world. Quit feeding your mind with lies. You will find that in the long run you will be a much healthier and happier person. The Bible has a lot of great advice. Some people figure things out on their own but only after years of painful avenues and dead end streets in life. The Bible is the best road map to life that exists, read it.

The Bible really is the handbook or manual to your life. It's kind of like the manual for your car. Yes it's there, but you never read it. You can still drive and get around, but if you took time to read the manual you would discover there are a lot of features you did not know your car had to help your trip be a lot easier. The Bible will make your life easier because of the wisdom you can acquire from it. Read it and learn from it. Then when you encounter situations, you will know how to react, saving yourself from more painful avenues.

The Bible is so full of truth and knowledge that many governments and wealthy people in the past did not want the masses to know what was inside. There have been many, many attempts to abolish it, burn it, completely get rid of every Bible ever printed, etc. but all attempts have failed.

The slaves were kept as illiterate as possible by the bad slave masters so that they could not read the Bible and get knowledge from it. However, there were good slave owners that actually taught their slaves to read so they could get the truth. Many of them studied the Bible with their slaves. If slaves could not read, they did not have access to the truth except by someone telling them. If they could read, they could depend upon their own skills and read the truth for themselves. Education became a goal for many slaves after slavery ended. They realized the value of being educated and many strived and worked very hard to get there. Schools were eventually built for Blacks. Now days, many Blacks – especially Black males- are illiterate and do not care at all about education. They see drugs as a way of life instead and kill each other regularly. I am sure if slaves from the past saw their descendants today, they would all be sick and would probably rather remain in slavery rather than let their descendants fall into such a horrible existence.

I know I covered a lot of different ideas here but in summary, the biggest idea to carry away from all this is that words and ideas are destructive to cultures, people and society... but they are most destructive to you as an individual.

Take care of your mind and your physical health as much as possible and you will feel better and live better. Get rid of all the media and sources of destructive thoughts so that your brain can reboot and you can live a better, less stressful life. Love others and treat them well, even if they treat you bad. You are now aware that if others treat you bad, their brain just "has a virus" of bad information and they are reacting to you in a preprogrammed way that they have been taught. You might be an influence that will help them wake up out of their chaos and blind disorder because you will not react as they have always been taught you would react to whatever it is they just did to you. They may grow to respect you.

In fact, you might loan them this book or just buy them their own copy so they can work on reprogramming their own mind. Everyone needs to deprogram in today's world. With the electronics of today, information can be so addictive. Just try to eliminate as many media sources as you can, but if you cannot completely eliminate media, then keep your sources as clean and true as possible and avoid the negative and the news.

CHAPTER 04: THE DREAMS

The government has an agenda. So do the wealthiest people in America. They have the same agenda. This is because the rich pay money to get laws passed in their favor to get The Agenda one step closer to reality. Part of The Agenda is to get rid of as many Whites as possible. Why? It is because Whites always mess up and delay their ultimate goals – The Agenda. What is The Agenda? Well, we will get to that later. We will first discuss why the wealthy have any agenda at all.

Most poor people think that if they only had money, all their problems would be solved. They are right. If they had money all of their problems would be solved. Let's be real about it. Most poor people have a need for food, let alone their wants and desires of a nice car, maybe owning their own home and other such things that they will *never* see in their lifetime.

Poor people live in a false reality. They have to blind themselves to the actual reality because if they don't, they would probably go insane being conscious of the reality of their situation. It is much easier to live in a fantasy world called "the Land of Hope". In this false land, the poor person imagines their self one day in some distant future getting to the point where money is not much of a problem. They might not have a lot, but they will be comfortable. They are retired and don't have to get up for work anymore. They live in a cozy home that they worked for and have a decent supply of money coming in from a retirement fund and social security (since they worked most of their life building society and keeping things going in whatever role they worked in). They are out of debt. They can travel with their spouse around the world if they really desired. They enjoy getting to visit their children and grand children and have plenty of money to help them financially if they need it. But their children probably will not need the help because they were able to send their children to the best schools and Universities when they were growing up. Their children will have a better job than they ever had a chance to have.

This vision is wonderful dream but is a complete lie. Here is the actual reality of poor people. Poor people in America will never be able to retire. They will literally work until they die. Social security will not be around much longer, but even if it is – it will not supply even half of what a person needs to live so will not do much good anyways. The government already destroyed the idea of family, so many people will die old and alone because their children will not want to even speak to them. Instead, they may count themselves lucky if their children even think enough about them to put them in a nursing home where some stranger will look after them until they die.

Most Americans will never get out of debt. They will die owing money and their family will have to do whatever they can to pay for the debts after they die because, even though the person is dead, the government has now made it the legal responsibility of the children (or whoever was named a beneficiary in a will) to pay the debt of the parents through a process called probate. Taxes to the government are one of the first things to be paid.

Traveling for the poor person as they get older will not be an option either because their health will be so bad from eating the unhealthy, chemical treated stuff that people call food that they will not feel like going anywhere but to sleep. And the idea of having a loving spouse by their side through it all is the biggest lie people live in today. The idea of marriage has been completely annihilated. There are literally almost no couples that stay together today for a life time. In fact, most couples divorce within a year or two. After a divorce most people just float around from partner to partner and/or remain single. Some give marriage another shot, or maybe 3, 4, or even 5 more chances with most of them all ending just as badly as the first.

With all this happening around us one must ask... what in the world is going on? What has happened to the world? It all goes back to The Agenda.

I just explained how poor people imagine their life to be someday and then the reality of how it truly is and how it will be in the future. Now I will explain the wealthy and their views on life.

Wealthy people start off in life with a whole different reality than poor people. Wealthy people are not in debt. They owe no one. They don't want to owe anyone. Instead, they want others to owe them. They can buy absolutely anything they want at any time. In fact, they seek out unique and overly expensive things – in other words things that are more of a challenge to purchase or obtain.

It must get really boring for them to go where ever they want and be able to buy everything in the store if they wanted to. In fact, they could buy the store itself if so desired. They have lots of friends and family near them all the time and will have all the way through until they die. In fact, they try to get rid of people around them. They know that most of everyone around them are fake and are only around them because of their money, but that really doesn't bother them. They just see it as another regular living expense to throw big parties for friends and family and it just helps to make them have a bigger, more powerful image.

Wealthy people spend their life traveling the world and enjoying its bounty while they are young and after they retire they will continue to travel and enjoy life because they have had the best care and doctors that money can buy. They also have had a virtually stress free life and have only eaten the best of quality top-grade food.

You see, wealthy people like a challenge. This is because things that are challenges for poor people like finding a job and getting food to eat and working their entire life to avoid becoming homeless are not any worries that wealthy people have ever had. They have absolutely no challenges and this makes life a little too easy for them – a little too boring as well.

Wealthy people don't have to try to make or keep friends. Wealthy people don't have to find a job. Wealthy people don't have to worry about bills or payments. Wealthy people don't have to worry about losing friends or family when they age. Wealthy people don't worry about food or shelter or anything of that nature at all. Wealthy people basically have no worries when compared to poor people. They have enjoyed all that life has to offer and they can have it all at any moment again and again. So, wealthy people don't even think about material things because they can have all that at the snap of their fingers.

So what does a wealthy person focus on? Wealthy people want power and legacy. They want to change things and they want to be remembered. Wealthy people want other people to want to be them, but never want those people to succeed at becoming anything even close to them. Wealthy people want their name on a building. Wealthy people want others to worship them. Wealthy people want others to say "if it weren't for you, I don't know what I would have done. I owe you my life".

Wealthy people want other people to owe them. Wealthy people want to have respect everywhere they go. Wealthy people want to know that they changed the world, and they want the world to realize it too. Wealthy people want their names in history books. Wealthy people want obscure things – many times not physical objects (they already have that) but sometimes it *is* physical things.

However, they are more likely to want ideas – like fame, recognition, power, and impact. Wealthy people cannot conceive what it is like to be poor nor do they want to. Wealthy people do not look at poor people as being human. Instead, they look at poor people as being born servants to their desires. Servants that do all the necessary work in the world. Wealthy people don't socialize with poor people – they look at them as being dirty, nasty animals that should not be touched.

Wealthy people don't like to do physical work. Wealthy people don't even like to come up with ideas – they will hire someone (a servant/poor person) to do that as well. In fact, wealthy people's biggest skill is management of other people and ideas. They know what they want to get accomplished and they pick the right people for that job. The wealthy do not personally do the work it takes to accomplish their goals themselves.

Wealthy people even hire people to manage their money and make it grow so that they become even wealthier. The wealthy don't like it if there are others who are wealthier than themselves – so they remain in competition with other wealthy people constantly trying to outdo each other for the top spot. They try to shock each other by finding something that is either unheard of or very difficult to obtain. This helps them feel more important.

You can begin to easily see the difference in the life of a wealthy person as opposed to a poor person. They live vastly different lives, have different objectives and motivations and see life through completely different lenses.

If you were to take a wealthy person's money and power away and put them in the permanent shoes of a poor person's life, I am sure they would certainly commit suicide. They would not be able to handle the life a poor person is forced to live through.

They also would see how they could have helped so many poor people with their money and power but never did. Instead of buying yachts, helicopters and personal jets they could have bought thousands of people homes and paid the taxes for all of them for a lifetime. They could have fed the people for a lifetime as well. I think it would make them sick to their stomachs once they truly realized this. However, they will never realize this because they will never be poor – and they will do everything in their power to make sure they never are.

So what is The Agenda of the wealthy person? Their agenda is to control. They want to control as much as possible so they can get the most recognition as possible. Let's think for a moment about history. Think about every single famous person in history books. They all did something to control or gain. Many of them are written about as the companies they ran. Here are just a few examples to think about. Let's begin with McDonalds…

McDonalds is probably the most famous fast food restaurant in existence. They brag about their success – billions served. It started off in California as a small restaurant owned by two brothers with the last name of McDonald. They were successful in the small area where they lived. Their food was good, the concept of a fast food restaurant was a brand new idea and everything about it was totally exciting.

However, you never hear about the McDonald brothers much because they did not make the business what it is today. Even though the store carries their name, they were actually run out of business by their competitor – Ray Croc. Croc bought the rights to their restaurant (the name, the food and the whole concept). Part of the agreement was that the McDonald brothers get to keep the original restaurant they were currently running, but they could not build any more locations or do anything beyond that one restaurant they were already operating.

Ray Croc took their idea and began copying the restaurant all across the nation – making the food look and taste the same at all the restaurant locations he built. Eventually, he built one right across from the McDonald brothers' original restaurant and took all their business so that they were forced to shut down! Ray Croc gets all the credit for McDonalds. His name is in the history books as being the great man with the idea – even though it was not his at all. He just had money and power to take it to a bigger level. Don't worry about the McDonald boys though – Croc paid them fairly well for it.

Another figure in history books is Adolph Hitler. Yes, he was a horrible man – using his power to destroy instead of build things up or make them better. But he was a wealthy man with a lot of power. He did extraordinary things that most people could never get accomplished in several lifetimes. He is secretly elevated in the eyes of wealthy people today because he was able to accomplish so much in such a short time.

He made people do things they normally would have never done. He brainwashed the citizens into accepting and even help promote all the things in his agenda. He did this so well that he actually had family members murdering their own family by burning their bodies and throwing them into large graves and furnaces as if their bodies were just trash that was swept up off the street! Can you imagine?

Most people don't even want to think about this as a real happening because it is so unbelievably cruel and torturous. However, since his rule, the United States has copied most of his brainwashing techniques and the United States even hired his top people to work for the US government right after the war with him.

The United States government carried on experiments right here in the USA on American citizens that were just as cruel as Hitler's inhumane experiments for many years after – sometimes resulting in the person's death. So Hitler holds large spots in history books because wealthy people see him as a hero.

While a poor person reads about Hitler and thinks, "Oh my gosh! What an evil and cruel man", wealthy people and high level government rulers think "How was this man able to accomplish this? I want to know his secrets so that I can repeat that here in the United States and get my place in history books." Hitler the hero is how he is observed by many.

Now you should be to the point where many things that have happened in the world are beginning to make more sense now. You should be starting to see why the wealthy and the government never do much to help out the poor. You can understand why they have different values and ethics. Poor people want wars to end. Governments and the wealthy want wars to continue for as long as possible.

Now you have a better understanding how America is separated ideologically between the classes of wealthy vs. poor. In the next chapter, I will discuss how America is also separated by Blacks and Whites and the reason for the Black and White separation.

CHAPTER 05: THE DAMAGE

Blacks and Whites are separate and will be for a long time to come. Has it always been this way in America? The answer is no. In the days of slavery, as we discussed earlier, slaves were Black but there were also White slaves that were referred to as "indentured servants". Blacks were considered to be farm owners' "property" so that if they escaped the owner could "reclaim" their property from "Joe Shmoe Farmer" down the road if he tried to take the slave as his own or if the slave ran away. Since slaves were considered legal property, the owner had the right to go get his slave back.

Also, if the slave done damage to another farmers property or something, they could go to the owner of that slave and make them legally liable for the damage since the slave was the property of that particular owner. As stated before, some slaves were very happy with their new life here because it was better than the African life they had before. But other slaves suffered and hated it here and would choose death over life here.

Some slave owners were Black. So you had a lot of extreme things happening among the various farms and settlements here. It wasn't one certain way. Some farms had tiers of slave treatment where the top tier slaves got to be inside the owner's house while the lower tiered slaves were out in the field working outside all day. This actually caused inner separation, jealousy, and even hatred among the Blacks toward each other. This separation still exists today. Many of the slaves in the homes became lovers with the owners and had mixed babies. The mixed babies had lighter skin. Today, you still see darker skin Black people hate lighter skin Black people. These are feelings that will not go away easily.

In the battle for wealth, the bad owners who were beating slaves were losing out financially. So the battle for ideas among the wealthy began. Was slavery a good thing or a bad thing? These wealthy people hired the best people of the day to work on marketing campaigns promoting their ideas and agenda. Like I said, wealthy people cannot stand other wealthy people out doing them. They always want to be on top.

Financially, the owners who were good to slaves were doing much better financially. When the bad owners tried to stop them by changing the rules of the game (from the owner/slave relationship to a new employer/employee relationship) and the good side did not listen, it eventually went from being a war of words and ideas to a war with canons and guns (the Civil War). The bad slave owners would kill to win.

The bad owners knew that they had to have a new concept to replace the slavery concept as a method for running their business. Therefore, they hired a team of people to come up with the idea of the employer/employee relationship that we have today. It is the same idea as slavery except with minor differences that we discussed in earlier chapters.

So here is another good example from history where wealthy people told the government what to do. They wanted things to go their way, so they got the President to sign a document to have the war. They acted like they were doing it for the betterment of people, but they were actually doing it out of greed.

You see, the President could have just signed a bill to make slavery illegal instead of going through a huge war first, but the government never acts when they have wealthy people on opposing sides asking them to do something. The government waits to see which side will pay them more money. As it always plays out, they will go through a war until they feel enough money has been paid, and then they will end the war with the resolution being for the side that paid the most money.

The government and wealthy people both want control of all the people that they can possibly control. They would love to rule with an iron fist – whatever they say goes. But this is a hard thing to achieve – especially when so many White people are educated and will fight against a government. Blacks tend to not fight against a government. Slavery is one example of this. Slaves outnumbered their masters by the thousands and could have easily killed the owners and took over the farms and had an entire new country for themselves. This did not happen... why?

It did not happen because Blacks do not tend to see the big picture. They get caught up in all the details of their lives and events. I don't know why this is, but it is a fact. Look at Blacks today. What are they concerned about? Some minor details that mean nothing to anyone except them and their friends. They have almost no worldly outlook on life… no big picture things they worry about.

Whites, on the other hand, focus on the exact opposite. Whites miss the details of situations and see them as non-important because they are focused too much on the big picture. They ask questions like "ok, yes this is horrible that this little thing has happened to me, but how is that going to mean anything a week (a month/a year) from now?" Whites watch the government and wealthy people and even though they do not have a lot of money, they will stand up against the wealthy "bullies" by protesting or fighting or whatever it takes to win. Wealthy people hate this. (By the way, White people of today are no longer like this much because they have been systematically changed by the government and wealthy)

Here an example of this in the days of slavery. The slaves would not fight to get out of their slavery situation. Instead they were caught up in the details that don't matter – like who "got to be inside the master's house" and who had to work in the field. They just focused on little details that didn't matter later.

In the mean time, Whites were focused on the big picture. They saw the bad owners who were beating slaves and saw it was wrong. They saw how this would negatively affect Blacks years later and if not changed could result in a bad situation to where Blacks would not even think of themselves as human anymore. That is the big picture.

But Whites did not stop by acknowledging the big picture… no. They actively tried to do what they could to help. They were poor and could not pay to get laws changed, but they could start a secret society of houses to help the Blacks escape to a place where they would not be found and would live safe. This later became known as the Underground Railroad.

The Wealthy people were extremely upset about this and so they had to figure out a way to stop all this cooperation and help among the Blacks and the Whites. So they set into motion things to make them turn on each other. Information that was wrong… information that was lies! They put advertisements and word out to cause separation between Whites and Blacks. They caused them to turn on each other instead of helping each other. They made Whites and Blacks begin to hate each other because of skin color and tone!

As you know, this is still here today. If you were to ask a Black person why they hate Whites, they will say because of slavery – even though slavery ended nearly 200 years ago! This is again them getting caught up in false details. They hate Whites for no real reason. But the same is true to a certain extent with Whites today. You can still find Whites who hate Blacks for no reason. If you ask them why, they will say because they are bad people who steal and kill and live off of the government for free and refuse to work... they are lazy! Is this really true? Yes it is. Blacks do kill. Go to any "hood" in a major city and see how many die each year from murder by a Black person. Do they steal? Yes like crazy! Do they live off the government and try to not work? Yes – you bet! However, this is changing in the world today. There are more Blacks working today than ever.

But now the question is: Do Whites do the same thing? Yes they do! You can see Whites who are lazy and live off of welfare for generations. There are Whites who kill and murder just like Blacks. Today, the line of separation is blurring. However, this is only among uneducated Whites and uneducated Blacks. Educated Blacks are seeing more opportunity as the country is becoming more populated with Blacks, while educated Whites are feeling pushed out, and even exterminated by the government. The question here is why? This idea is what we will explore next. Why is it that Whites are being sidelined in America, and what are Whites to do about it?

The remaining bit of middle class Whites (not wealthy but also not poor) are leaving the United States by the boat-full. This is not because they want to travel; it is because they know what is coming for Whites in the near future in America. They are leaving permanently. The trend in the United States over the past few decades has been to take away more and more from Whites and to give more and more to Blacks. Blacks can get a free college education, free food, free brand new housing, free birth of babies, free doctors of all kinds, free dentists and more. Blacks are getting the best of the latest greatest jobs, getting all the fame on television, and have now even taken Presidency.

Whites are being pushed down, left behind, and taken advantage of. White culture has been crucified in the media so that Whites are embarrassed to act White. So now, you have White youth that are very convincible as being Black. I sometime have to take a second, third or even a fourth look – and still may not know for sure if the kid is White or a light-skinned Black.

The days when Marty on Back to the Future was the prime example of a White youth are gone. The media has done a terrific job at brainwashing today's White youth into abandoning their natural identity. It is almost comical when I see a White youth talking with the voice of a Black youth, wearing his pants hanging down to his knees with a ball cap turned backward and tattoos covering his arms from top to bottom. The boy actually thinks he *is* Black. Sometimes you want to just slap the young man and tell him to snap out of it but you know it is way past too late.

The young White women are doing the same thing. They talk the talk and walk the walk.

The other part of this is that the White youth of today are very uneducated. Many of them cannot read. They are getting lowered down to the level that slaves in the past were at. In the days of slavery, slaves were often kept illiterate so they could not read information to get educated. If you are educated, then you get a chance to rise up above the ashes and see the bigger picture of things going on around you, and you can then intelligently fight back or at least get yourself out of a bad situation.

The populations of Whites in the United States has gone way down (by millions) over the past few decades. The population is now so low that in the 2010 Census they changed the definition of who is included in the "White" count so that the number will seem bigger. They now count Latinos (Mexicans) as being White. It also includes people who reported "White" or wrote in entries such as Irish, German, Italian, Lebanese, Near Easterner, Arab, or Polish. This is happening because the government does not want White America to go into panic and do something to delay The Agenda.

This is a plan that has been well established decades ago – to destroy the "White" race both as a culture and as a people. Again, the reason why is because Whites don't sit back and take things – or at least they didn't used to. They used to take action and create changes through their numbers. The Black people actually had a few leaders that took actions and rallied people together, but that is where it all ended – just a bunch of talk. That is the way the government likes it. They want you to do "civilized protesting" meaning they set up an outlined area on the sidewalk where you can walk around and talk and hold signs up. Do you think this scares the government? Hell no it doesn't. They just laugh at those people and go right on doing what they were doing before those people arrived there. Why would they change anything just because there are people outside walking around on sidewalks? Let's get real.

There is a new system that is about to take order and the first place this will happen is the United States. With Blacks leading the way – you really are about to see *change*.

We now have a Black President. Blacks are waiting for him to make change, but what change is there to make for them – really? Today, Blacks have exceeded Whites in rights. Let me tell you my personal experiences with this. I went to college at the same time as my sister. We sat down for an entire summer writing out letter after letter trying to get scholarships to help pay for college. We sent out hundreds of letters over a period of several months. We only got a handful of responses back and all of them were denial letters. We wasted an entire summer writing and writing when we could have been out enjoying our summer together with family and friends before we left for college. It was sickening to go to college and working 3 jobs and taking out student loans to make it through school while nearly every Black person I met blew college off by partying and then would say, "I don't care about school. I don't want to be here anyway. I just had 3 different full scholarships to choose from and they are paying for it. I'm just here to have fun and party until they kick me out."

When I asked them how they managed to get these scholarships, they would tell me their counselor at school just signed them up. They were scholarships for "minorities". Since I was not a "minority", I did not qualify. The stupid thing was that almost all of them I talked to had several to choose from with each choice paying for all the years of their college until they graduated (a full ride). Each was for a different University so they got their choice among top Universities. I couldn't even get a single scholarship and neither could my sister! And we were top students too, making all A's and B's throughout high school.

If you don't believe me, all you have to do is look around for some scholarships and you will see that almost every one of them are for minorities. Just for fun, you should try applying for some if you are White, or just write on the application that you are White and see what happens. You will quickly see what I mean. The Whites of today are experiencing discrimination.

I now have student loans over $150,000 and they are gaining interest every day. I cannot afford to pay them because my job as a teacher does allow me to even cover my monthly bills. I will never be able to become a home owner. I will never be able to purchase a new car. I will live the rest of my life as an impoverished, but educated White person. My sister is right behind me along with countless other White people.

Almost every single Black person I went to school with had a free education and walked out of school into a high level job position their first year making more money their first year than I will ever make in a year of my life as a teacher. Why is this? It is because the government has structured it this way on purpose. Not only are scholarships aimed at Blacks, but jobs are too. The fact that Blacks are getting all the best jobs and getting a free education to boot is because they will do whatever they are told. Just like the Jews from the Holocaust, they will do what they are told to simply keep their position. It is back to the idea of the Slave that is in the "House" vs. the slave who is in the "field".

When Barack Obama was running for Presidency, all you ever saw in the media is Barack Obama. He always had a smile on his face, he was always making promises of "Hope", and he was always appearing to be the "good guy" who was looking out for everyone. It just seemed like you couldn't go wrong with this guy. He always had charisma and charm. His wife always had a friendly smile and seemed good-hearted.

On the other hand, Hilary was always being made fun of in the press. She was always portrayed as someone who could not handle the job and that if we were to hire her, we were actually hiring Bill back. Bill even helped this image along by appearing at most of her events and talking for her.

Then there was Sarah Palin. She tried to act as dumb as possible. Everyone in the nation, even the dumbest of the dumb people, wondered, "How in the world was she picked as a candidate?" She always seemed like she was drunk or something. She fumbled her words. She said and did the dumbest things in interviews. John McCain was the same way. This man was so stupid acting that he was an embarrassment to Whites. He always called himself "the Maverick" and then claimed to have been having conversations with an imaginary friend whom he would refer to as "Joe the Plumber".

If you don't see what I am talking about, you really have been badly brainwashed and are in dire need of recluse from your television set. For those of you who are smarter, you will quickly be able to see that this was all an elaborate setup to purposely get Obama elected. Who else could you have chosen? There was no one even close to appearing as smart and together as Obama (and he really is a smart man).

Now that he has been elected, what has he done? Well, let's start by what did he promise? He said that the very first thing he would do is end the war as soon as he got into office. Did he? No. In fact, he created more war than we had before and increased the budget for war immensely. He is just doing as he is told to by big business men as has always happened in the government. It is nothing new, so it really does not matter who you have sitting in the seat of President, they will always be corrupt. And guess what… if the President does try to do what is right, they end up dead. *JFK.* So why did they pick a Black man for President? It helps the Blacks all across America to finally side with the government because since they are now a majority, they are going to come into play in the next stage of The Agenda. So what is the plan? Read on to find out.

CHAPTER 06: THE DISSECTION

The government did a lot of major work from the 1960's all the way through modern times toward The Agenda. So let's discuss some of the key things that took place in this time frame – not in big detail, but just brush over some main ideas.

In the sixties, there were certain White people with a certain lifestyle we now call Hippies or Flower Children that were involved with a particular movement and lifestyle. There were both Black and White Flower Children but it was mainly Whites. Jimi Hendrix was one of the famous Blacks from this movement. What was this movement all about? It was about freedom to do whatever you wanted. People were having sex outdoors in front of each other. They were having orgies and sharing partners. They were doing all kinds of drugs – LSD, or acid, was one of the biggest drugs being used. People's minds were being warped from one end of the spectrum to the other.

The government created this culture by allowing the drugs to be put out there and then allowing them to circulate freely around society. People attended concerts, like Woodstock, doing drugs and having sex with multiple partners. It was a time in which the government encouraged lust and self pleasure. A government always has more power over people when the people get away from God. This was a generation they encouraged to get away from God and into their own lusts.

The government had a plan to destroy this entire generation and began working to do that when the people of this generation were still of a young age. In 1962 and 1963 the government banned (outlawed) prayer in school. All the decades and centuries before this, teachers prayed with their students in prayer to Jesus every day – and this was in public schools, not just religious schools. Outlawing prayer to God in school was just the government's first step in destroying the moral foundation of this generation and generations to come.

Then throughout the sixties as this generation grew older, the government passed drugs throughout the population of the youth and encouraged them to "think freely", without the limits of God. They also put the country into the never ending war of Vietnam (notice they were working on this one particular generation by upsetting their psyche). This was the beginning steps of the planned destruction of White America, and it worked very successfully.

The government also worked on this particular generation to become proactively involved politically. This generation ended up being more politically involved in laws and lawmaking than any other generation because they were programmed to be. Why did the government want them to be so politically involved? Because they could lead this mind-scattered generation around like a mouse in a maze, get their votes, and change the laws to hurt citizens and advance The Agenda. The government could cause them to vote on particular laws that they wanted passed through the use of advertisements and mind control. However, in America, you had to be age 21 to vote. So to get a bigger voting pool more quickly from this generation that they had brainwashed and destroyed mentally, the government lowered the voting age from 21 to 18 in July of 1971.

The government began working *immediately* on a law through which would further destroy the moral fabric of this generation. They would pass the bill into law with the new voting power of the Flower Children themselves. With some afterthought, the government decided that this idea they had for a law would be better to go through the judicial system instead of creating a bill to be voted on. When it would go through the judicial system, no one would have to vote for it... it would automatically become law. The law would not be overturned because this generation had been demoralized and the government knew they would readily accept the new law. What law is it? Keep reading.

They got an inside undercover government agent to become friends with a pregnant girl named Norma McCorvey. The agent talked with Norma and got her to think about her life in terms of herself – especially in terms of her "rights" as a woman. She told Norma that she shouldn't be forced to have a baby if she didn't want to. It should be her decision as a woman to be pregnant or not. She made Norma feel angry toward the man who "got her pregnant against her will". Norma, being a person with a weak mind was easily swayed and fell for it. Norma agreed to file a lawsuit against the State of Texas so she could "have her rights as a woman" to kill her baby if she wanted to. However, Norma did it under one condition – that her identity not be revealed. The officials agreed and gave her the false name of Jane Roe. Texas, being one of the most conservative states, did not go for this craziness at all and shot her lawsuit down in flames.

This is exactly what the officials wanted and this was their prime opportunity to move a step closer toward The Agenda. Instead of just making it legal for a mother to kill her child in Texas, they took it all the way to the Supreme Court so it would now be a Federal law that all states would have to follow – not just Texas. That way, all women across America could begin to kill their children before they were born and it would be completely legal.

In 1973, when this same generation was old enough to have kids, the government passed the law giving the right for women to kill their unborn children (abortion). This was something that was unheard of in America before that. How is it that people were able to accept this? Again, with drugs distorting their thoughts and sex in open streets people got confused and questioned their own reality as to what was really real. The introduction of the abortion law was just another thing that added to the confusion. Some people began to wake up while others went into deeper confusion about things. In general, people continued down a path further away from God – some further than others.

Many years later, Norma got older and wiser and began to figure out she had been brainwashed to do something she did not really want to do. She blew the cover of her secret identity she had been given and told the world her real name. Norma also told the world how she regretted helping to get such a horrible law passed. Norma said she found Jesus Christ and became a Christian and now saw all the wrong she had caused. Norma wanted the law reversed and thought if she came out and said something against it herself that it would be done away with, but it was too late. There were women all over the United States now that believed it was their "right" to kill their child if they wanted to. The Agenda was now another step closer.

Now, in schools, they began to teach White youth that it was a bad thing to have babies. They would teach them to use birth control as well as condoms so that there was almost no way they would have a child. They taught the White youth that "they don't want to have a kid and mess their life all up." These youth began to agree and said "yes, I want to have sex, but I don't want to have children. Therefore, I will do as you say and get on the pill. And like you say, he might have a disease since we are all doing drugs and having sex with each other so I will make sure he wears a condom too."

Now this still wasn't good enough. The government wanted to decrease the population of Whites much more than this. So in the eighties and nineties, they started pushing forth the idea of abstinence (not even having sex at all). This would be the "only way to fully protect yourself". Protect yourself? What is it we are teaching our youth? We are teaching them that it is wrong to have babies. Today, you have 30 year-old Whites having children (that is if they do actually go through with the pregnancy and have the child) then they give their child to their parents to raise because they don't deserve that kind of a "burden" on their lifestyle and after all, they are just "too young" to be a parent. What kind of nonsense is this? We teach the youth that they can never be trusted with any kind of responsibility and it has now hurt the White population dramatically. There are fewer Whites in America now than there ever has been. What little amount of Whites that remain are getting dumber and dumber. I think we could say the White race in America is in emergency status.

Now let's look at the other side of the spectrum. Blacks were taught differently. They have been taught that they can go out and have unprotected sex all that they want to. They were not taught that they were too young to have the responsibility of being a parent – no! They were taught it is their responsibility to be a "Baby Mama" where they have multiple kids with multiple men and the men to have multiple children with multiple women. The common age for Black youth to become parents are around ages 14-15. This is considered normal in the Black community and culture.

The entire Black culture of today was manufactured and then advertised through the use of MTV (Music Television), BET (Black Entertainment Television), and other sources and this is still being done today. They are taught how to think and how to be (how to live). The main idea is that they have as many children as possible by having sex, sex, and more sex. And don't worry about the cost because the government has them covered. The government covers the full cost of having a baby for Black people (a full ride).

On the other hand, White people must get insurance to cover their costs of having a baby. But even when they have insurance, they probably are not covered for pregnancy – but they don't find that little detail out until it is too late, meaning that they have to pay for *all* the costs out of their own pocket. So when the costs of having children are put on Whites, it puts a financial strain on their entire family and the family then puts pressure on the young White couples to "not have any more kids because we can't afford to pay for and raise your kids too".

The White culture was put on MTV in the eighties (when MTV was first invented). This entire culture was manufactured as well. Just look at some of the silly videos from the eighties. They look really dumb. But Whites enjoyed them at the time and copied it into their own fashion and everything because it was something brand new and exciting. When a new Madonna video came out, the style of outfit she wore in the video quickly hit store shelves so that everyone could buy it. In fact, they may not have had a choice to buy much of anything else – so they were kind of forced into buying it, but they didn't mind as much since everyone else was wearing it too. They would just wear a handmade accessory to try and make their outfit unique.

After the eighties was over, the wealthy-driven entertainment industry began to focus more on the manufacturing of Black culture and began to make fun of the White culture they had manufactured the decade before – laughing in the faces of those who really had no choice but to dress and adapt to the culture that was dropped into their laps. This made Whites hate themselves and begin to adopt the "new" Black culture. White boys who listened to rap music were labeled by other Whites and Blacks as "wiggers", meaning "White niggers". This hurt at first, but then as time went on and rock 'n' roll died, rap culture came to center stage. The "rockers" became the ones who were made fun of and the "wiggers" became mainstream.

As time progressed into the first decade of the 2000's, White culture (what was left of it) virtually disappeared while Black culture became more refined and into public acceptance as the norm culture. This culture is now widespread everywhere in all settings. This is the culture you see in people at the club, at the mall, in grocery stores, in every minimum wage job (you even see McDonalds workers "sagging"), and even in the office at professional work environments among people who are supposed to be "supervisors" and "superiors". The Whites in America went from being a group of people that wanted to help Blacks to become equals in society, to a society where Whites are begging Blacks for acceptance into society.

There is now a 2-mode style of communication that has developed (originating out of the Black culture). This 2-mode communication is basically "ghetto" talk and "professional" talk. Let's explore… If a person is in a situation where they are expected to be professional (aka: people above them in the job ladder are watching them perform, present, or do something for the company) then they put on a professional appearance (vocal tone, body language, etc.) in perfection without missing a note.

Someone watching from the outside would think that this is a well-educated person who carries their self professionally throughout all aspects of their life.

However, they don't know the reality. Any other normal day at work is like being in "the ghetto". The talk is there, the body language is there, the vulgar behaviors and topics of taboo conversation (inappropriate in a work setting) are there and this is all because that is who the person identifies themselves as being – whether they are Black or White – skin color or tone doesn't matter anymore.

To put it quite bluntly, there is now one culture in America and that is the culture of "dumb". If you do not fit into that category you are quickly rejected socially. Who really cares if you get rejected you might ask? You do if you want to keep a job and feed yourself and your family. I'm just gonna label this culture of new workplace behavior as "blacktude". This "blacktude" is everywhere as we mentioned before – probably including your superiors. Now don't even try to "act ghetto" because they will see right through you. These people have such a strong clique and intuition of who is in and who is out that it is impossible to break in and be accepted – even as just a casual co-worker. They don't want you as a co-worker, they only want others like them around. Don't think you can go sit in the corner and just come in and do your job and get out because it isn't going to happen, they will make sure of that. After all, "you might just be with the po-po".

No, you just went through college hoping to have a professional job where you could be around other educated people. Not anymore... at least in the United States. Blacktude is becoming the strongest form of prejudice in this century – outdoing color prejudice, outdoing racial prejudice and outdoing age prejudice… you can be of any age, color, or race, but you have to have their values if you want to remain an employee there. If there was a governmental order for you to be put into a concentration camp, it would be one of these people that would put you there and keep you there. Unfortunately, this is about 70% of society now. If you are reading this and know what I am talking about, you already know as well as I do that we are in some serious trouble.

So what are their values you ask? Their value is placed on status – number one. The higher your status within the group the better you are treated and recognized. The next value is treason. They will stab you in the back the first chance they will get. You must be street smart to survive inside this group. If you are a generally good person who treats others as you want to be treated, you will not survive, and will not be accepted. They will have you cut up so much by performing what they call character assassination on you, that you will walk away not even knowing for sure who you are or were.

Their value of treason evolved out of decades of street life with drugs and weapons, untrustworthiness, no parents, parents on drugs, doing drugs, selling drugs, violence, murder, imprisonment and homelessness. Then, all that mess was taken by the government with your tax money and put through free education and into careers that your children should have had as CEO's, CFO's, directors and every position level within the company. Now businesses comply with Affirmative Action so your kid is the one without a job – or maybe it is you without the job.

OK mom, so now you are beginning to understand why your 40 year-old son with 3 college degrees is sitting in your living room playing with his newest game console/ cell phone/ computer on unemployment with no hope of returning to work. It is not just an entire generation of Whites who are losing at the game of life… it is White people altogether from this point forward. Wake up! That's all folks! It is sick to think about what will be happening in the next 30 years when the baby boomer generation is gone. They were the last generation to know anything about White people having a financial chance in America. Those days are dead and gone and I would be willing to bet if you asked any of them they would tell you all about it.

The Baby Boomer generation was smart in a lot of ways, but in a lot of ways their generation is the one that was majorly responsible for the swift financial and technological changes that has happened over the past 30 years. Their generation was handed everything on a silver platter. From toys, to cars, to education, to jobs this generation paved the way for all future generations.

There was a fundamental difference in the Baby Boomers from their parents' generation before them. Their parents' generation looked into the future and tried to guide society toward what was better for everyone. The Baby Boomer generation looked at the future and guided it toward what was best for themselves.

Some evidence of this is the fact that when the Baby Boomers went through college and graduated, there was a business man that gave them a good job with lots of responsibilities. This was good because the Baby Boomer was taught how to run the company while the person above them faded out and retired into a good life, leaving the Baby Boomer to run things from then on.

However, the Baby Boomers are so self absorbed that when their children came out of college during the eighties and nineties, they didn't have any jobs for them except low-level, low-paying jobs with little or no responsibility. They pushed the idea that they must "work their way up" from the bottom or else they do not deserve the higher positions. They never turned over responsibility because they wanted to keep the high paying job for themselves. In fact, if you were to take a survey of the average workplace today, you would see that the Baby Boomers never retired! They are still in the position of authority at the top today!

If you were to ask them why they are still working – it is not because they are in desperate need of money – no! It's because they either are greedy or maybe they retired years ago but came back because one of two reasons: One, they were bored, and two, they had not properly trained anyone to take their place and the company could not function without them.

The Baby Boomer generation likes it this way because they like everything to revolve around them. They like having a company not knowing how to run without them. In fact, that is where that term came from: "the world doesn't revolve around you!" That is a saying that came about because of the Baby Boomers. They really don't like to see others succeed more than they. They want it all for themselves. They have a lot of greed. They have... pride.

That is the Baby Boomer generation's downfall. Now, of course, as all ideas in this book, this does not apply to absolutely every single last one... but it applies to so much of a majority that you can say it that way and be correct in a general sense. Even though the Boomers played a huge role in all of this, it really is only one piece of the puzzle. But you might be starting to see that White America was not necessarily demolished by Black people. White America was demolished by White people and it continues today.

CHAPTER 07: THE DESTRUCTION

For planned destruction of any kind to happen in any society and be successful, one must first make the society be as weakened and demoralized as possible. This means taking the society as far away from the Christian God as possible. As stated in the last chapter, this started with taking away prayer in the schools. But they didn't stop there. They replaced it with the "Pledge of Allegiance" – a daily morning prayer that all students say in union to a cloth flag representing the government. So prayer did not stop – they just changed who you pray to. This pledge was already put into place so that everyone would be used to it when they banned prayer. In fact, thinking in advance in their plan, they added the words "under God" in 1954 so that it would sound more like a prayer and to make it sound like the United States is God.

The next step of removing God out of American society was the twisting and perversion of what was meant by "separation of Church and State". The original meaning was to keep Church separated from government so that the government could not pass any laws against Christianity – such as banning it. They did not want a government where God was removed out of power in society because they knew from the past experiences that this would cause destruction to the nation and the people.

However, the changing of the meaning came into play and they tried to make it sound as if it meant that Church was not supposed to trump government – that instead of religion being the guiding law in society –

government would now be the governing law in society. They effectively took the law and reversed it through a play on words.

What happened after that? Well, not just the removal of prayer from schools but also the removal of the Ten Commandments from government buildings. There has been an ongoing battle to get the words "In God We Trust" from being printed on money. These are just a few examples but there are many more.

The idea of the separation of Church and State is one sided and only benefits the government, but it was originally meant to be partial to Christianity. If there were differences, disagreement or conflict between citizens and the government then the Church would be the authority and make the final ruling and would be protected from the government trying to overrule it's authority in society.

Today, because the courts have twisted the meaning, in times of differences, disagreement, or conflict the government now overpowers the Church in authority. This is a huge fundamental change from how this country was first established and set to run. There used to be separation between them so that Churches (being the House of God) would not have to pay taxes (on the money they brought into their congregation, sales taxes, property taxes, etc.). That would be wrong. It would be like the government charging God money to have His Church here.

But guess what? Yes. Churches now have to pay taxes to the United States government as well as local and state governments. But, I thought they were separate? Not when the government is going to benefit. They suddenly are seen as though they are together enough for the Church to owe the government instead of being separate.

Basically, the government has placed itself in authority over God. Now obviously, this will not last. As we Christians know, it is just a matter of time before this government will fall because God only tolerates such undisciplined and unruly behavior out of anything – including people, governments, animals, and yes even Angels – for a limited amount of time.

God does not allow any sin to go unpunished. If He did, then He would be lying to all of us and everything He has done would be completely unfair to everyone – including Jesus. Could you imagine Jesus saying "What? You mean I actually didn't have to die after all because everything was just a lie?" Can you imagine how upset Jesus would be? That is right. Everything happening will eventually end with progression of time as promised by the Messiah. Maybe we should try imagining the President/government official trying to get into Heaven and Jesus is standing at the door and says "No, sorry. You cannot enter." The President/government official replies "Excuse me! Do you know who I am? I am (such and such person)! Now let me in! I did all kinds of things for you on Earth like spoke at charity events and well…. We even had an Easter Egg roll every year on my lawn!" And Jesus says something like "Go to Hell! I never knew you! You might have done such and such things, but your heart was full of lust and sin and you did things for the world and the government… not *me*… therefore, depart from me and go take the punishment of the second death for yourself. I am not paying for you!"

Wow! Can you imagine? And from my understanding of the readings within the Bible, it really will be something similar to that! Look up Matthew Chapter 7 Verses 21-23.

Now there are battles attacking everything in society that is Christian. In the nineties, all of the Flower Children generation that had done so many drugs, had unprotected sex and orgies with as many people as possible, and basically lived about as an immoral life as you can imagine had children that were now becoming teenagers. They taught their children in a very different and immoral way from any other modern generation because of their own past experiences. They taught their children nothing about God. They taught their children that they should do whatever "feels good" to them and then directed them down the same immoral path they were on. Evil was the underlying principle that was taught and ran the gamut through all things life for their children. The freedom of explicit and immoral sexual expression and use of drugs was also taught – if not directly, then indirectly.

Their children infiltrated schools like an army with a whole new way of thinking, being and living. The biggest game changer and impact that these two generations made together was the idea of mainstreaming homosexuality – one of the biggest abominations to God that you can do. When their children went to school and became gay and lesbian, teachers and staff took notice. As soon as it was seen that these children were getting treated different because of their "sexual preference" there was instant lash back from the parents. The parents did all kinds of immoral and sexual sin when they were young and by damn you were not going to stop their children from doing the same thing!

Because this Flower Children generation was now in the working world and in positions of government (again part of The Agenda was to get this drug infested generation to actually spend a lot of time and effort in their haze-filled world trying to get laws changed to make their sin be forcefully accepted by society) they were finally able to make laws and get them passed that say you cannot discriminate against someone who is gay – meaning you have to teach them, you have to hire them and now you have to let them in the army too.

These people took the nerve to compare their homosexuality to that of the slaves who got beat by bad masters! Can you believe that? Unfortunately, that was just a seed they planted. Now it has gone way out of control to the point that they have gotten laws changed to make it ok for people to get married to someone of the same sex. It is very obvious that these people never had any moral values of any kind taught to them whatsoever.

You have to stop for a minute and ask yourself… isn't it weird that the government you pay your hard earned tax dollars to are making laws to tell people who they can or cannot stick their penis into? I know that is graphic, but honestly? With all the murders, and theft, and gas prices out of control and everything else crazy going on in the world, lawmakers decide to focus their attention on this? What kind of a government are we pledging our allegiance to? Have you ever stopped for just a moment to ask yourself that?

Demoralizing society has been a lengthy but planned process. It is crazy that some young gay man can go get his boyfriend put on his health insurance, but I cannot even get my uninsured mother put on my health insurance.

Speaking of health insurance, this brings up another piece of the control. Insurance started out as a simple mafia ring where hit men would go to local business owners and make them pay money to them or else they would destroy their business (burning it, etc.) or hurt the owner physically (breaking bones etc.). This eventually turned into a completely legal business operation called insurance – a contract where you pay money so no bad thing will happen to you. If it does, you get some of your money back.

One law that the government successfully passed is the law that you must pay car insurance. Even though you live in a free nation, you do not have a choice about this. If you want to drive a car, you have to cough up part of your paycheck to an insurance company every month. Health insurance has always been optional – meaning if you don't want to buy it, you don't have to (which is the way it should be for *all* things that cost money). But now, Barack Obama has successfully passed a law so that in the near future, health insurance will no longer be an option either. You will have to cough up more money every month to them for health insurance. This means you pay lots of money every month out of fear that something bad might happen to you. Wouldn't you rather be able to go shopping once a month or be able to give your child a little money when they need it? Instead all your money is going to insurance companies.

Now, when you go to the hospital or doctor, the insurance company tries their best to not pay for your "bad thing that happened to you". They tell you that every year *you* must pay the first xxx thousand dollars. Then after that you must still pay for 20%-40% of the amount that they must pay. Basically, you end up paying out of your pocket for most if not all of the doctor bill!

Then after that (even if they paid nothing for you) they increase the rates so that you pay more each month just because they want to. So now you end up not only paying for all the bad things yourself, but now you must pay them more money as well because a bad thing happened to you. Even worse is that you have no choice. What kind of a deal is that?

Tell me one reason why you would even want insurance? I hear you. What if... What if that "one big thing" happened to you where you really need the little help of the insurance company? You know, like a major thing where someone dies or something. Now I ask you, how often does that really happen in your personal life and how much do you think you could save up in the bank if you put the amount you pay in insurance premiums each month into a savings account that draws interest? Do you think that maybe the savings account could cover some what-ifs? I would bet that it would. And also... I forgot... you are White aren't you?

Black people really don't care about insurance or insurance laws because for a majority of them it is free. If they don't have the free insurance and something bad happens to them, they just go to the emergency room where they cannot be turned away for any reason, get "fixed" and then they never pay the bills if they even get one. They get the same care if not better – because after all it is an emergency – even if it is just a little sniffle that some Tylenol will clear up. I know that some of my Black readers are laughing right now because they have either done this or know someone close to them who has.

But there are some other readers out there who are flabbergasted. They did what!!!! Yes, that is why the emergency room is so full that when someone has been shot, they cannot get seen. Real emergencies get overlooked or forgotten in the mix sometimes. I know there are some medical people saying, "Well no, we got code levels. When they come in, we rank them and something more severe goes first." Yeah, you are right. That is, after they get done with the people who are already taking up the rooms. They have to get them out first, then clean the room, and find a doctor who knows how to deal with a more severe case. By the time all that happens, the person could be well on their way to death. So are you upset? Of course, and you should be!

Well, if that wasn't enough to upset you then just wait till you hear this. I used to work at a bank years ago. I saw all the accounts of the customers. They would have me look up their accounts, tell them how much they had, and then they would ask me for financial advice. As time passed by I began to see a trend. There were many older customers that were millionaires and many others who were close to it. They all had one thing in common – healthcare costs. I am not talking about going to the doctor. I am talking about nursing home care, community living, or private in-home care.

These customers were paying outrageous amounts of money for care. There was one customer in particular that I remembered. His wife was in a community living situation because he was too old and brittle to take care of her. She was in even worse health than him and desperately needed the daily care provided there. He was paying over $30,000 per month! I was shocked! I had to have him repeat it because I thought he had to have said $3,000 a month, not $30,000! But he was right. I saw it being automatically withdrawn each month. He was very bright mentally and I don't believe he was being swindled. That was the real rates of their services.

He had about a million dollars left. He was trying to figure out how many months he could afford to keep her there before they were completely broke. This was their life savings they had built together.

I began to see couple after couple with similar situations. I got to admit, there were times I thought about telling them to pay me the money and I would take care of them and just quit my banking job, but that would have been unethical and I could not have taken their money like that... it just seemed wrong. What do you think about that? These people were married their entire lives together and saved up their money, all just to be taken by some business at the rate of nearly $1000 per day. I think that is sick!

OK, so let's get back to God and look at just a couple of more things that government changed in relation to God. We talked about how they made it *OK* for gay people to get married. But that doubles as an attack on marriage itself. Marriage is a Christian idea. Adam and Eve were married by God Himself and He made a commandment that Christians should get married and have children – one man and one woman. That has been changed by man now.

The reason God set up marriage the way He did was because it provides stability. Can you imagine having two moms and never a dad? Or what about two dads, but no mom? How would that feel? Weird....... People that are gay or lesbian should not try to promote their lifestyle at all. They also should not be able to raise children, point blank. They are not normal. They are not *OK*. They are not born that way. They are not to be accepted. No... don't go too far the other way... they are not to be killed. They are not to be abused, threatened or beaten either.

These people are just simply people with an addiction... a lust that they cannot control. They may not realize it is something to be controlled. Let me give you some examples. A person begins gambling all the time and loses all of their money. They end up homeless. Should the government say they are too big to fail and give them some tax money so they can gamble it again? Say what?

OK, if someone really, really loves to have sex in public places in front of passersby's, should we make a law that allows them to have sex where ever they want? If a thief just loves to steal and they do it all the time but they get caught, should it be made legal to steal so they can continue their lust openly? If a murderer just loves to murder and they just keep going to prison, should we change laws so that they can freely go out and kill?

If people just love to cheat on their spouses, should we change the definition of marriage to mean it is *OK* to cheat within that marriage? Uh oh! I think I heard some of you saying yes to that one. Better go check yourself.

The further away from God that a government can drive its population, the more control they can have over that population. I mean it can get to the point where a government is telling who you can or cannot sleep with – oh sorry, we are already there aren't we? (The government says "You can sleep with and even marry someone of the same sex if you want to, and we will make sure everyone in the entire nation accepts it and caters to it.")

Maybe I have uncovered your blind eyes just a tiny bit more than they were. Maybe I haven't. If Church and State are separate, then why are there any laws at all about religion? They are supposed to be separate so government should not be making any laws about religion whatsoever. Why are teachers getting fired for just saying the word "Jesus" in class? Does that even make logical sense? I mean even to a non-Christian, does that make any sense that someone could be fired for saying a name? However, if teachers teach about Buda or Judaism or any other religion besides Christianity they get props. Why is that exactly? Why are Christian holidays being pulled from the school calendars year after year, while other religions holidays are being added? Are we starting to see a trend here? Is it a trend, or a plan?

CHAPTER 08: THE DEMANDS

I think we have begun to see that the government is all about control and power. Governments of any kind through all of human history always have been. Why do we have governments? How do governments get created?

Let's think about the world before any government was created. Everyone is living and working together just fine with no problems. But then a person here or a person there does something to hurt another person because they somehow gain from it.

Eventually, the general population of people become crazy (murdering, theft, etc.) and it becomes difficult to live in a society filled with those kinds of things. Therefore, there has always been a group of "good" people rise up and put some sort of an established ruling into place. What that means is that they create laws to say "if you do this bad thing, then here will be the result and/or your punishment."

For example, let's pretend someone killed another person. There was already a law established to say that if you killed someone, then anyone and everyone who could capture the killer could encircle the killer and throw big heavy stones at them (ouch!) over and over until they died. Great! That sounds like a good solution.

The hope is that everyone will be so afraid of getting stoned to death, that they will never kill anyone. However, one day, there is someone dead and there is a suspect of who did it (maybe because they were having a disagreement with the victim just before the death occurred or something). Then they find the suspect and get ready to stone her. But she cries out and tells everyone that it was sincerely and truly an accident. She really did not mean to kill the victim. They were struggling and the victim fell off the edge of a cliff.

Now, does she get stoned or not? Don't even let your mind go there! Does she get stoned to death or not? This is where societies get confused. So they end up with different sides and views as to how this matter should be handled. This is how the court system got established.

With courts, you are not supposed to be considered guilty until you go through a hearing and are found guilty by the court. This is where some chosen people have been placed in higher authority than normal people in society (judges for example). They are put in charge of making these kinds of decisions (is she to be stoned or not?) That way, there is some standard system that everyone is supposed to adhere to whenever crimes are committed.

Otherwise, you would have situations where the family of the victim would just go and kill the woman who may or may not have actually murdered their family member. Then, in retaliation, that family would go to the other family and murder someone back and then it would be a continuous circle of murders back and forth (kind of like the Hatfield and McCoy's you always hear about).

This kind of back and forth justice is prevalent today in Black neighborhoods where gangs run rampant. The killings usually start as a result of drugs, money, or both. In fact, some of these neighborhoods (in New York City for example) are so dangerous that police are not allowed in after a certain time of night! That's right. The police have a curfew!

It is hard to turn sin around once it gets rolling. That is why governments try to get as much control as possible. However, as time goes by, the government gets more and more control over your everyday life. Instead of taking care of crime and making society a peaceful place to live in, they start telling you silly things like how fast you can drive your car, how much money you have to pay them each time you get any money in your hands (taxes), they tell you that you cannot walk around in certain clothing (or no clothing at all), they tell you how to raise your children, if you are a farmer, they tell you what kind of seeds you have to buy and from whom to buy them, they tell you to come and gamble at all their facilities (lottery, casinos, etc.) but then tell you that you cannot start your own lottery because they know it is wrong.

They force you to get shots when you are young against your will, they can make you take off your clothes at airports, they can shoot or taser you if you look "suspicious", they tell you that you can no longer leave their country (and their government system) if you owe past child support or if you don't have a passport, then....

Wait just a minute! Does that mean you cannot leave the United States without a passport? That is 100% correct. This "free" country has you locked into its borders already – just like Germany did the Jews in the days of Hitler. Oh come on... it's probably always been that way. No, this was a law just put into effect in 2007. What is this all about? Now don't go getting all claustrophobic on me. You can still breathe... can't you? Welcome to pain and suffering. Welcome to... The Demands.

The government is only good up until a certain point. This is the biggest reason why all governments of the past have either failed or been overthrown. Once they get to where they are intruding in your personal life, they have gone past the point of doing their function of protecting citizens and have gone to the point of hurting citizens instead.

Here is a very simple example in the world of today. There are speed limits all over the country. The reason this law is in place is to "protect people from accidents". The punishment for speeding has usually been a speeding ticket. The cost of a speeding ticket was not much at first, just enough to make you think twice before speeding. However, now there are some places charging over $2000 for a speeding incident!

The latest gimmick of "law enforcement" is more than a speed trap. They have cameras set up with computer systems so that if you are speeding as you pass by, it takes a picture and video of your car and close-ups of your license plate as well. Within a week or two you will receive a speeding ticket in the mail!

There are some problems I have with this. First of all, if they were really concerned about the safety of people, instead of issuing laws to write speeding tickets, they should issue laws on car manufacturers to make a car not operate over 65 or 70 miles an hour. The cars I have owned usually register up to

140 mile per hour! There is no speed limit in the United States that allow that kind of speed.

With computer and GPS technology, they could actually control cars so that they will not go faster than the speed limit for that particular area and automatically adjust for school zones and everything. Then there would be absolutely no speeding. If someone "hacked" their car to override this, then they could be sent to prison.

I know, now you are saying "wait a minute, I wouldn't be able to speed!" Exactly! If that is a law that we want, then this would be the way to make it happen. If it is not a law that we want, then we need to remove speeding law from the books and allow people to drive at whatever speed they feel comfortable with (which is what happens anyways – even if there are laws against it).

A government's biggest sin against its people is its growth. We need a government to stop crime and punish those who commit crimes.

However, we need the crimes to be serious things only like murder, not silly little things like whether we can say the word "Jesus" in school or not. In fact, the founders of this government were aware of governments who got too big for their britches and gave the people the ability to abolish the government for cases of this nature.

In the past, every government has failed because of reasons similar to this and the people effectively tore down their government and made a new one that worked better for them. However, today, because of the advancements in technology, we have entered a new time and day – where a government is "too big to fail".

The United States has so much weaponry and technology that if citizens were to even try to take them down, they will attack back with such a massive and bloody proportion that they could literally kill everyone in the entire United States (or the entire world for that matter) if they so chose. The United States government will never fail and they will never go out of business. That is what makes our situation unique from all past governments. The United States will never allow its people to take them over – period. In fact, if you were to even try, they will label you as a "homegrown terrorist" – meaning that you will be targeted for torture in multiple ways that I will not get into – just search the Internet or read other books for more information on people who have already tried.

A government's objective is to grow. It all boils down to money. If I (just plug in the name of whatever governmental organization you wish) get 1 million dollars from tax payers this year to spend on my mission, but I really didn't need all the money. Then, at the end of the year, I am going to spend like crazy on whatever I can think of – just so I use up all the money. That way, next year, I can ask for more money (maybe 2 million dollars) and tell them that I spent every last penny last year and that we are a growing organization with needs.

Now, the organization gets $2 million of taxpayer money. So that organization hires more people and purchases more buildings. Now next year they will need $4 million, because they have more employees to keep jobs for and also have more expenses (more building, etc.). This cycle never stops and the United States Government is a professional at keeping this cycle going.

Now they not only use up every bit of the taxpayer money, but they borrow even more money from foreign governments just to cover their "expenses". So the government is basically taking out "Payday Loans" so they can have more money now for themselves.

Where I come from we would call this a con artist, charlatan or a swindler. They are not out for our best interest, but out for their own. Somehow your pockets get emptier while their pockets swell out bigger. In fact, the United States government's pockets swelled so big that money was pouring out where all the businesses around them noticed.

So the businesses went to the government and said "look, we can destroy you because we are powerful enough. We have the resources. But we don't want to do that. We just want in on the game. Tell American citizens that our businesses are "too big to fail" and that they must give us xxx billion dollars by Friday or else it's going to be the end of the world for all United States citizens! I said do it now! ...or else." What a wicked world we are definitely in!

CHAPTER 09: THE DISORIENTATION

The world has changed drastically in the last 100 years, especially in the United States. My parents grew up in a totally different world than I did. My grandparents grew up in a world that was so vastly different from mine that I cannot even conceive of what their experience was even like and vice versa. But before that, the world was largely the same for centuries before and there was very little change that happened over huge spans of time.

Back then people could live and die in the same reality with almost no changes in their life and the society they lived in. If there were any kind of changes, even subtle ones, it was a huge event for them – one that got written down in history books and stories told about it for decades and maybe even centuries to come because change was just simply something that very rarely happened.

Today, there is so much change (especially culturally) in the United States that aging people in their early 50's are finding that they have to try and learn the culture that exists around them because it is totally different from what they know. They are experiencing culture shock in their own country in the same places they have lived their entire life! The culture and things they once knew are now dead and gone.

Today, things are changing at an even more drastic pace. The culture is now a culture of change itself where nothing stays the same. People are no longer loyal to anything because things will be different tomorrow and that includes marriage and their thoughts (and maybe even their personality).

My cousin's 19 year-old daughter got married to a guy and two months later, she got divorced! She is not a unique story this is happening to almost everyone today. Barack Obama's campaign was also won on the idea of "change". When can we stop changing?

Is there anything going to remain the same for even just a little while? The answer is no. Why? Things will not stop changing until the government gets things where they want them. Where is that? Things will begin to stabilize out when the government has total control over the citizens and the citizens are totally dependent upon them. Scary! I hope I am dead and gone before then but I probably won't be.

So how is this ongoing plan being pulled off so secretly? Well, it is a story that has gone on for generations. All the things we have discussed so far are the things that have led up the condition we are in today. There are so many people from so many different agencies, and so many different time periods involved that it is hard to point your finger at one group of people or just one organization and say they are the culprit. It has been a collaborative effort among many different organizations and many different people over various time periods. However, this group is much smaller than you think. At the top of every organization, you will have only one or two people who run The Agenda of that organization.

You want to think, well why would someone keep an agenda going from people who are now dead and gone? Because The Agenda is not one that is tied to a specific person, it is one that is tied to a specific idea or theology. The next person that comes to power keeps The Agenda because it now benefits them… not necessarily the dead person, not the retired person, or basically not the person who used to be in their position (or at least not directly). Just like most of us are taught in school that we will be an employee, they are taught that they will be a ruler – a king of some sorts. They are taught that you belong to them as an employee to do their will.

People are not seen as people. People are seen as an idea. For example, who is the one man over our country? I bet you said the President and you are right... the President... not some person who lives down the street from you, but The President. We see people as a position, as a thing... not as a human (even though the media has tried to show a more human side of Presidents lately – for example, President Obama buying a dog for his kids.)

When someone dies, we don't say this is the guy or gal who spent extra time with me and made my life better for such and such reason. Instead, we say, this person was a graduate of xxxxxx University, they were the committee chairperson of xxxxxx Corporation or school board, or they were a cashier at xxxxxx store. So and so was a great parent. You see, we view people as their roles, not as the people they really are.

When we die, the first question that people have is, "well who is going to get so and so's job now?" And usually there is someone there waiting to jump right in and things will continue as is (with a minor bump of adjustment). The dead person is quickly forgotten about as ever existed (except by a couple of people who really were close to them).

So how did we get this numb and cold as a society? You might even be asking me right now "What do you mean numb and cold?" You may not have even seen anything wrong with the above described picture I just presented to you. You might just say "Yeah… that is life, so what is your point? What does that have to do with numb and cold?"

However, there are many of you that are saying "I know exactly what you mean and I can see exactly what you are talking about." Well, if you are one of the people who are saying that you don't see anything numb and cold about people being seen as a role instead of a human, then you are part of the problem because you are someone who has been so brainwashed that you cannot even *feel* anymore. You have a lack of sympathy and respect for others and you probably have been told this before somewhere in your life (maybe from an ex).

However, this is not your fault. You are a result of a program... of The Agenda to make you as detached from your feelings, love and especially God – as possible. What! That's right. You are brainwashed and it might take some work on your part to snap out of it. That is why I suggest you stop all media flow into your brain. Your brain has been overloaded with messages from media sources on how to think.

One example is the weather report on the news. They tell you what the weekend weather will be and then will suggest activities you should do. Why do you need someone from an electronic box to tell you this? You can look outside and see the weather for yourself and if you practice at your own observations, you will find that you will be even more accurate than the reporter on guessing out the weather.

Then they also tell you activities that you should or should not do. Again, why do you need this? Even though it might only sound like "a friendly suggestion", this suggestion has a much greater impact than you think. If they tell you it is a great weekend to go grill out, you start thinking about it. Then you say to yourself "Yeah, I'm gonna grill out!"

Then when you go to the grocery store you will find that as soon as you walk in the door they are ready for you with huge racks of drinks, hotdog buns and chips right in the middle of the aisle by the checkout line! How coincidental and curious? This is not an accident. The news folks (as nice as they are) are paid (well, the station is) to do these types of things. It was not a coincidence!

You will notice that many of the "surprising" or "shocking" news stories are exactly the same year after year. They could actually just pull last year's tapes out and just replay them. Here are some example stories to watch out for… in the summer watch for stories like "Record summer temperature highs are causing gas prices to go through the roof!" and during the Christmas shopping season… early in the season: "retailers are worried that they won't be able to make enough sales. Shopping is down and it looks like it could be a bad year for retailers. The government says you should go spend your money now so that it will help kick start the economy."

Then a couple of months later: "Retailers had one of their best shopping seasons yet! Customers were rushing into the stores only to find their (favorite new hot toy) has been sold out. So and so store says there will be no rain checks issued on that item."

Here is another favorite thing I like to hate about shopping: You see an ad in a local stores weekly ad for something like a television for xxx amount of dollars (way below the normal price). So you call in just to check before driving there, and they tell you "Well, that is what the ad says. I would hurry up and get down here because we only have xxx amount of them and they will go pretty quick at that price."

You begin to get the idea that the employee may buy it for themselves and quickly rush into the store to get yours. When you get there, you look at the shelf and it is stocked full and has a much higher price. You ask someone who works there about the one in the ad and they tell you "Oh that was a misprint. The real price is so and so amount." Your face turns red with anger. They tell you "there was a sign outside by the door when you first walk in. Didn't you see it?"

Well, the point is, now you are in their store and they hope you will go ahead and buy the item anyways and many people do because they already envisioned themselves owning it and they really want it bad now, so they pay the extra price because it is, after all, $15 cheaper than normal. But if you pay attention, you will notice the same store has "misprints" often.

OK so numb and cold... The reason people are so numb and cold today is because we are taught to be this way by the government and schools. Schools, by the way, are the training and brainwashing grounds of a government. If you want to see what I mean, research a different country's government and school curriculums because you can separate yourself from it. In other words, you didn't go through the brainwashing of that country, so when you see it as an adult from an outsiders perspective, you can see it more for what it really is.

Just for kicks, search the Internet for some words like "Nazi propaganda for school children Hitler coloring books" or go websites like these examples:

http://www.nizkor.org/hweb/people/m/mills-mary/mills-00.html

http://en.wikipedia.org/wiki/Nazi_propaganda

http://library.duke.edu/digitalcollections/vica/

Also, try going onto www.google.com and typing in the search box "Hitler with school children" and then when your results pop up, click on the "images" link at the top left corner of the Google page and you will see nothing but pictures. You will see many pictures of Hitler with children trying to look like a "good guy" in his preparation of the people to support his massive murdering and destruction that he would soon be doing.

All things start with an idea. Hitler had an idea and now he had to brainwash people into getting behind him on his idea. He wanted all sides of the political spectrum to come together to support him, he did not want to just be backed by his own party. He wanted to appear like a good guy with good intentions and he had an idea for change… a change for the better... a change for our youth to have a better future than us. But also hope for ourselves as well. This is was all it took for the people to come together as one and support every idea that Hitler came up with including mass murder of thousands and thousands of people.

One basic principle that a government uses in gaining total control is the idea of separating a person from their self. If a government can get you to think of yourself as a product or as a position instead of as the human being that you are, then they gain more control. How? Well you will do things that you normally would not do if you have no feeling of remorse or humanness inside yourself. It is like telling a young woman to get an abortion. They try to make her believe that the baby is not a human... it is just a thing growing inside her – like a cancer. They make the girl believe that it is just a simple medical procedure to get this "thing" removed out of her body.

The girl is brainwashed and blinded and decides to go through with it while in this mindset that has been given to her. She doesn't think twice about it at first because her mindset is one of thinking about the baby as a "thing" instead of as a human. She is also thinking of herself as a "thing" instead of as a human. However, as her life unfolds through the years, she will likely at some point come out of the influences of this brainwashing and will begin to see the truth of the reality. She will realize she murdered her very own child. She may want to be in denial for as long as she can, but eventually, this will likely hit her very hard emotionally. She will probably need counseling or some kind of support to put her own life back together again. She will realize that not only did she kill her child, but she also killed a part of herself that will echo throughout the rest of her life.

Many times the father does not even know that he would have been a father, but many times he does. The sad thing is he will hurt just as badly, but he has absolutely no choice in the matter. If a woman wants to kill their child, she legally has that right. What if a man wanted to have the abortion, but the woman didn't? Could she be forced into it against *her* will? Wouldn't that be fair to allow the man to choose as well?

Abortion should not be a *choice* for anyone. It is so sad to see nothing being changed legally with abortion. But, a government likes it this way, because they gain so much control over people when they make them think of themselves and others as a product.

The government teaches you that life is about things and that you are just in the mix. They teach you to think logically (which is not natural). They teach you to think of yourself as a product. However, the real and natural way a human functions is by emotions and feelings. Think about the smells, emotions and feelings you had as a child. Mom or Grandma making homemade rolls etc. Smells, emotions and feeling are very connected to each other and strongly affect a human spiritually. Sound does too but not as much as these other three.

Sight is more disconnected from the feelings than any other sense. Therefore, the government promotes a world that revolves around vision (eye candy) because it causes humans to get further and further away from the truth of their own spirit and natural being. God made us flesh, but also spirit. We have natural spiritual intuitions that God gave us. The government of man will refer to these things as unexplained phenomenon but God explains it as spiritual gifts. These are no mystery to God because He created them in us.

One example of a spiritual intuition or gift is a situation like this: the next time you are driving down a busy street or highway, I want you to pay attention to yourself and others more closely. You will see that you can actually know when someone wants to change lanes. Even though they do not put a turn signal on, even though you never saw the driver's face, even though the driver never slowed down – basically with absolutely no changes to indicate this idea, it is as if you read the person's mind and thoughts to instinctively know that they wanted to change lanes.

Maybe a couple of minutes (or maybe within seconds) the driver will make the move you thought they would. How in the world do you know this? You will find you spend almost every moment in driving reading the thoughts of other drivers around you and predicting their actions in advance without even thinking about it.

You probably know exactly what I am talking about. If you don't know what I am talking about and this sounds like a bunch of nonsense to you, then you are probably the person that is always causing accidents. If this is you, then think about it and be honest, how many accidents have you had? Also, you are probably so out of touch with yourself that it isn't funny anymore. You are one that thinks of yourself as a product. You probably don't believe in anything spiritual because all your own spirituality has been robbed from you through the technique of brainwashing. You are probably such a logical thinker that you think your entire life out in steps, and then when something gets out of alignment with those steps – you get psychotic and possibly full of rage and/or resentment toward others. This is because your reality of yourself and everyone around you as being a product has been proven wrong and your mind doesn't know how to handle it. Humans are not naturally logical.

Now, allow me give you an example of this. A particular guy has his thoughts set straight (logical thinking) so he knows exactly what he wants for his life. He thinks "*OK*, I am going to marry this particular woman and she is going to be this such and such way our entire marriage. She will not change. I will not change either. I will continue chasing after whatever other goals in life I want to and she will always be there by my side because we are married. That is the meaning of marriage after all. It means that we will go through life together and that's the end of that."

Well, that is fine and dandy, but as soon as this guy gets married and his wife now wants things to be this way or that way, but that is not in his vision or plan, then he will not allow it. The wife, thinking in a logical manner as well, goes and does things that her reality tells her to do anyways. This causes disruption and problems in the marriage. They both start to get psychotic because neither one of them know how to handle situations that don't go as specified to their logical reasoning and pre-made reality.

They start to argue and fight, and each of them tries to tell the other why they are wrong. It *is* wrong in their eyes because their reality will not allow something different than the prescribed plastic life brainwashed into them. Neither one is flexible and neither one has feeling for the other.

Things get bad very quickly and they end up divorced. They did not love each other. They loved their own ideas of "marriage". But "marriage" takes two people. They wanted someone to make their logical idea of marriage to feel real. Because neither of them had any true feelings for each other to begin with, they separate and they both get a new boyfriend/girlfriend within a week or so. It is as if the marriage never even happened!

You see, when you are trained to think of yourself and others as a "product" or a "thing", as opposed to the spiritual being that God really made you to be, your life becomes really shallow and empty. The sad thing is you probably don't even realize that you are shallow and empty. You may start to feel depression someday though. When you do, you are again encouraged to think of yourself as a "thing" and to just take a pill. This will help that "malfunctioning brain" of yours!

The real reason you are depressed is because you are a spiritual being and you need to express yourself in a spiritual way and you also need to "feed" your spirit with spiritual things. This is why God said "Man shall not live off bread alone, but off of every word that proceeds out of God's mouth." This is God telling you that not only do you need to eat food daily to live a healthy life, but you also need to read and/or hear the Word of God daily to be healthy in a spiritual sense (depression is a spiritual state, not a brain chemical). In case you want to read some places that talk about this in the Bible (King James Version), here are some references:

Deuteronomy Chapter 8 Verse 3:
And he humbled thee, and suffered thee to hunger, and fed thee with manna, which thou knewest not, neither did thy fathers know; that he might make thee know that man doth not live by bread only, but by every word that proceedeth out of the mouth of the Lord doth man live.

Matthew Chapter 4 Verse 4:

But he answered and said, "It is written, Man shall not live by bread alone, but by every word that proceedeth out of the mouth of God."

Luke Chapter 4 Verse 4:

And Jesus answered him, saying, "It is written, that man shall not live by bread alone, but by every word of God."

What these verses from the Bible are saying is that you can do nothing without God. If He wishes, He can take everything away from you in a moment, or He can give everything to you in a moment. But no matter what your situation is in life (with all of its ups and downs) you need to be in Him daily and thanking Him daily and most importantly, getting to know Him daily by reading the Bible. This is the only way to get to know about who God is. If you expect to have eternal life with Him after you die, you had better start forming a relationship with Him now by getting to know Him.

So you might have depression and bad things happening in your life. You probably need spiritual nourishment. Maybe in school or at work you need to take a moment in the day and say a small silent prayer to God thanking Him for guiding you and asking Him to be with you as you go through life. You also need to do things with your family or friends that are healthy and spiritual. Go outdoors and take a walk or go have a cookout where you actually gather up wood from the forest and cook on that instead of charcoal and other chemical junk. Get as close to nature as possible and get away from the electronic world that the government and business tries to keep you in. You are not an electronic item. You are a spiritual and Godly being. Start drinking more water and less carbonated chemical-filled drinks. You are not meant to have these things in your body.

When you start to see yourself as a spiritual being, it is weird at first because you have never perceived yourself that way before. It is foreign to you. You have never prayed or maybe you have never prayed with your boyfriend/girlfriend before. Maybe you have never been a leader in your home or in your life. Wake up! It is time for you to step up and take charge of your life and stop letting government and business live your life for you. When you just obey them, you are so easy to control. Like I said before, some control in society is a good thing. We need to keep people from killing each other and things of this nature. But when you get into controlling the aspects of how a person lives their daily personal life, the government has gone way too far and into areas they don't belong.

CHAPTER 10: THE DISCIPLES

Where is all this leading? What is the future of mankind? What is the ultimate plan? I am going to answer those questions in this final chapter. Now a quick review of the basics that we learned about governments:

• Governments were created by citizens to keep peace and order in society by holding people accountable for doing anything really bad like committing murder and stealing.

• Governments naturally try to take control over ordinary citizens that never commit crimes so that they can get more money from them.

- Governments naturally try to grow as big as possible until one day the people will get upset enough to overtake the government and destroy it.

- Every government in the past has failed because of the above problems. However, the government of the United States of America is now "too big to fail" and so are the businesses they support. Because of technology and modern weaponry, the U.S. government will never be taken over by the citizens. There is no one able to overtake them, so this is a huge difference from every government in all history. We live under a government that cannot be destroyed by anyone except God Himself.

Given this knowledge, we can predict where things are headed. The trends are already happening right now so keep your eyes open. The first thing listed on The Agenda for the past several decades has been technology. They now realize that technology gives them a massive amount of power. In the past they tried to develop technology themselves. However, in the

1990's they got the bright idea of having society to further develop technology. They could have citizens across the nation create technology for free and at really fast rates.

The Internet had been developed and used by the government since the 1960's. In the 1990's, they used the Internet to make the use of technology widespread among citizens. At first, only people who knew a little bit about computers began using the Internet, but it quickly spread to everyone.

The Internet explosion in the mid to late nineties started off as a fun and exciting place where you could meet people from all over the world and talk with them – mostly in chat rooms. People would discuss every topic in the book – usually things they could not discuss with people in the real world. Online, you could discuss absolutely anything and in complete anonymity (no one knew your identity). Back then, there was no such thing as creating an account. There were no passwords or user names. You just hopped on any computer in the world that had a connection to the Internet and started playing.

The major search engine that everyone used was Yahoo, and the absolute hottest website program was Yahoo Messenger (for chatting). Yahoo really had the market back in those days. However, Google came along and was a much better search engine and Google took almost all the value out of Yahoo except Yahoo still had the chat feature. Over time, all kinds of social networking sites began to appear including dating websites. Yahoo also had the market on this for a while.

The difference between a social networking site and chatting was that instead of getting on the site and talking through chat (which was in real time, person to person – like a phone call), you would create a page about yourself and there was a mailbox where people could write you and leave messages. That way, you could have some ongoing conversations that you could continue the next time you got on a computer. You didn't both have to be on the computer at the same time.

Your everyday person who learned a little bit about computers could really have an opportunity. If they could start a website that had a new cooler feature than everyone else out there, then they could take the market share of people. The more people coming to their site, the more fame they had and eventually (years later), they could make money from advertisers. That's right. Ads on the Internet were not even in existence online in the mid to late nineties hardly at all. Most businesses did not even have a website. The Internet was seen as a fad that would quickly fade out. The only ads you would see were for other websites – people helping others by connecting their sites together through something called "external links". Later, as more people were buying computers and using the net – businesses joined in quickly.

So more and more people began using the Internet. However, it started off mostly with what people consider to be Generation X, but old people eventually got into the mix – yes I said old people! They got into the game before younger crowd did. There used to never be high school aged kids and younger online. It was seen as a thing for people in their late twenties and thirties. So what attracted the old people? They could get online anonymously and talk to other people. Most of these people were in nursing homes and were really bored. This put a little excitement into their life. They would talk to random people offering life advice. They loved talking to people that seemed to listen to them. So more and more old people started learning how to use a keyboard and mouse and navigate the Internet.

Not long after, the teens started using it, even though it wasn't "cool" for them to be doing the same thing that thirty year olds were doing, but they didn't want to be shown up by a bunch of nursing home folks either! They did not want to be the only ones *not* using the Internet.

Once they started using it, things got really crazy. Bad things started happening. Older freaks would entice young kids they got to know anonymously through chat to come and have sex with them. There began to be a large number of teens running away to meet someone they thought was another young person (or sometimes not, sometimes they knew it was an older person) to have sex. This, of course, caused uproars.

The uproars caused more and more people to get curious about what this Internet thing was all about. So a new wave of people came on board.

During much of this chaos, you began to see websites start to have user names and passwords. Before this, you could just get on a person's email and read it. There was no password to keep it private. Yahoo was just something you got on without any username or password, but this all changed. Websites started forcing you have a username and then shortly after, they made you have a username and a password both.

When passwords first came out, you could see the password on the screen as you typed it. People sitting next to you, walking past your screen or friends looking over your shoulder could see your password. But most people didn't care. They would just yell out their password for everyone to hear. They would let other people log in under their account and look at whatever, pretend to be them, etc. because it really wasn't taken very serious at first. The Internet was just fun stupid stuff to do.

Later, the ****** for passwords came out and everyone hated it because you could not see the letters or numbers as you typed. You did not know what you were typing. Old people who couldn't half see would sit there for an hour trying to log in and would get very frustrated. They would ask people around them to help.

Nowadays, you would never guess that going online was that way just a few short years ago. This is because technology has changed so fast that no one can hardly keep up. Everyone is now using computers and people are going through college to learn how to program computers to work for businesses as a computer technician or programmer. There are literally thousands of people and businesses trying to one-up any kind of advancement that is out there by creating something totally new. There are another group of people who just improve on things that are already out there. These people have one or both of these motives – profit and fame.

This is what the government wanted. They don't have to pay employees to do all that work. They get everyday people and businesses involved to develop the technology at a much faster rate than they ever could have and the idea has worked tremendously well. They still have tech people working for them, in fact, the top programmers in the nation. They just use the development made by others and implement and build on the best of these ideas to further The Agenda.

I remember in the early 1980's, rumor had it that the government could see a penny on the ground and could read the year on it through use of satellites in the sky. I remember looking up at a big beautiful blue sky and thinking "no way". No one else believed it either. It just seemed impossible. But now anyone can do just that on their computer at home. With Google Street View, you can even see real views in three dimensions of all the streets in the United States and around the world by clicking your way through the streets!

Technology in all areas of the government have benefited by the advancements made by everyone. This includes their weaponry. The focus on the government in weaponry development has been to control large crowds. There is a weapon they have invented that will cause the water in your body (your body is around 70% water give or take a little based on your age) to heat up and make you to instantly feel as if you are in a very hot oven!

To get an idea of the effect of this just turn your oven on in the kitchen to about 500 degrees. Let it heat for about 15 minutes, then go into the kitchen and stick your face right above the door and then open it. The wave of heat that rushes out will almost knock the breath out of you! Go ahead try it! It will be something to take the boredom out of your evening.

This weapon was made for large crowds so if they were trying to overtake the government, they will instantly scatter trying to escape the heat wave. This weapon is called the Active Denial System. I wonder what they are actively denying you from? This weapon is already in use. Here is a website on Wikipedia about the weapon with pictures of it:

http://en.wikipedia.org/wiki/Active_Denial_System

This is just one simple example. I have heard about weapons they have in outer space where they could literally just plug in an address or GPS coordinates and send a hot laser beam down to instantly kill and burn anything in that particular location! This is unstoppable power and the government likes it this way because they have everyone under their complete control.

However, they are still thinking of every move you might make before they roll out their entire system. One option you might choose is to run. What I mean is you might simply leave the United States and go to a different government to live under better conditions. They already thought about this and fixed all the holes so you can no longer leave.

It is almost impossible to leave the United States today. They have "border patrol" where people are all along the border with guns. They are supposed to be there so Mexicans cannot get into the country. Now think about it. How many illegal Mexicans are in your town? That's right. It's free for all. These people are at the border in practice so that when this new system is implemented in a few years from now they will be there so you cannot leave. They already make you have to get a passport and visa before you can even take a vacation outside the United States – this now even includes the Caribbean Islands! Now that is control like never before. That is not something that will happen in the future, that is already here and in place.

They have heat sensing devices in outer space so they can see anything alive on the ground anyplace on Earth and watch as it moves. You literally will not be able to hide or run like slaves of the past did. There will be no underground railroad and there will be no way out.

Given this information, you may wonder why a government just doesn't go ahead and kill all of its citizens. The answer is that as much as a government hates to think about it, it actually needs the citizens to survive. If you kill all of the taxpayers, then where would you ever get all the money you need to exist? How would they buy all the expensive things they have? Who would make the expensive things they have? Who would they be in power over? If all the people are dead, they have no one to hold authority over – rendering them powerless. Remember, the government wants power, not powerlessness.

Imagine a picture for a moment of the government killing all of the citizens. A few weeks into the aftermath of it all, the President, Senators, and lawmakers and all the rest of their crew come outside to witness the wreckage. In the smoke and dust all they see are dead bodies and smell the stink of rotting flesh. They wonder who is going to clean up all this mess.

They are getting hungry too. They wonder when the food delivery truck is coming but they start to realize all the truck drivers are dead. All the farmers are dead too so there is absolutely no food being produced. There are no more nice cars being manufactured. No clothing. No more homebuilders (this one is a minor worry because they have a whole bunch of empty homes across the nation to pick from that went through foreclosure).

No more television or movies, no more Internet, no more creative ideas, no more... you get the point. Life on Earth would pretty much be over. They would live their lives out and that might be it. Renewal of life would start with any survivors that are lucky enough to remain and reproduce.

The government does not like that ending, so that is why it is not part of their plan to kill everyone. They want things to keep going as is, but for their life to be really good and yours to be really bad. They want it to go from an employer/employee relationship back to a master/slave relationship. They don't like it when employees start to think they are somebody and start making demands (like retirement pensions or pay raises). The reason they ended slavery was so they didn't have any of these kinds of responsibilities. They don't own you anymore and therefore are not responsible for your well-being anymore. They want to go back to slavery, however, because the employee has certain rights that have been gained over the years and they get paid way too much.

There was an example of this in Wisconsin in 2011. Union workers said their rights were taken away in collective bargaining. This means that their pay rate on contracts (teachers for example) from the State of Wisconsin is usually bargained for. They make deals with the State government as to what kind of pay they will get the next year or two. They usually hope to get an increase in pay and benefits, but that may not happen. That is why their union bargains with the State to make any changes. It may be a small increase, a large increase or maybe no increase at all – but pay normally would never go down.

Well, the Wisconsin government decided they were not going to bargain anymore and stripped all the union workers of pay and their rights. This is totally against the Constitution but the government has so much power today that they don't have to abide by the Constitution anymore.

All the government wants now is for people to work for no pay. They don't feel you are worth getting pay but they know right now you won't go for that, so they just tell you to do it anyways and call yourself a "volunteer" or do the work "pro bono" just because you are a good citizen. They have pay cuts and furloughs so that they don't have to pay you as much. They even cut jobs and let you struggle to survive while they sit back and laugh.

While you are out there working your butt off for free (volunteering, etc.), they are sitting back in their nice comfortable leather seat on their personal jet sleeping while on their way to a nice beach vacation! What a great life! I wish I could afford just one vacation in my life. You see how this plan is so perfect for them?

Now when it begins to get really bad here in a few years, they will have to have several very important things in place:

First, they must dumb people down as much as possible. This has already been happening for decades but more dramatically in recent years. If people are dumber, they rely on the government more for their survival and are more willing to do whatever the government tells them in order to continue surviving.

Secondly, they must make everyone as disconnected from their emotions as possible. This can be done by taking away interactions with friends and family in the flesh and making it "digital". Now instead of spending that much needed spiritual time together, you just text.

Even a phone call was more personalized than a text, but they made the idea of texting "cool" and then got everyone hooked. Now they just brought you a third degree away from the spiritual aspect that we as humans need.

The 1st degree was separating you by distance from each other. They made the world a "smaller place" by giving society planes, trains, and cars so they can live far away from each other.

The 2nd degree of separation they got from you was taking away the actual human being out of your life by just having you talk on the phone instead of traveling to and from their house.

The 3rd degree was taking the voice of the people you love away and giving you a text message – basically a digital note. This digital note now represents everything that person is to you. People are actually having social awkwardness and anxiety in social situations because they do not interact with anyone on a regular basis in real life. Isn't that crazy!

Anything the government can do to make you more separated from your emotions, feelings, and each other the better for them. As we discussed in previous chapters, this disconnectedness makes people feel more confused and it makes them become separated from the spiritual being that they really are. It makes them feel helpless and it definitely keeps everyone from uniting. Everyone will soon be disconnected from their real emotions and become completely dependent on the government and media for their feelings and emotions. That is a very powerful position to hold and actually we are already there – but it's gonna get deeper. So hold on tight.

Thirdly, they must take as much control as possible over each and every person individually. A big part of control begins with monitoring. The U.S. government now monitors every telephone call you make, every website you visit (they record your IP address of your computer – basically a social security number for your computer), they monitor every text and email you send, every comment you make on any website, any and all pictures you upload, all purchases you make, everywhere you drive (they use GPS units for this and also street cameras), and much, much more. All this information about you is being recorded and stored in a governmental database.

It does not stop there. They record the sound through the microphone in your cell phone and the video images from the camera lens on the cell phone even when your cell phone is powered off! The only way to turn this off is to take the battery out of your phone completely. But if you do that, what is the point in having a cell phone? They also track your location through your cell phone and also through the use of your credit and debit card transactions. They have even been storing every person's blood and DNA samples since the 1960's. As soon as a baby is born, the nurses take these samples and send them in where they will be kept for eternity!

The government has computers analyze all your data and they can fairly accurately predict where you are at any given time just by the patterns in the data. For instance, you go take care of your mother on the weekends because she is getting older. The computer sifts through the data and can predict that every Saturday about 8am you will leave your home and go to your mother's house. If they really wanted to, they could come to your house and plant a camera inside while you were out without ever leaving any evidence that they were inside your home. Then they could have footage of you from inside your house at all times as well.

This is supposedly already being done through flat screen televisions. That would make sense because they passed a law telling you have no choice but to get a flat screen and they stopped selling the old tube style TV's altogether. Why does a government pass a law telling you to change your television? Are we so blind we can't see what is going on around us?

It's kind of like making a Jewish person wear a big yellow star pinned on their shirt wherever they go. Did nobody think this seemed strange? The reason the German government made Jewish people wear the big yellow star was two-fold. First, it helped police to track them and secondly, it helped separate people in society (creating a new hate between people and causing them to separate and turn on each other). This is exactly what the United States did long ago with Black and White people as we discussed earlier.

Suddenly, no one wanted to be a "Jew" because there was obviously something "wrong" with them if they have to wear a big yellow star. It made others turn them into the authorities when the Holocaust started. The big yellow star is back except this time it's in the form of a cell phone. This is all the tracking the government needs.

At some point soon, we will see computer chips being implanted in people's bodies. It will be in their hand or arm. This will be a chip that will track absolutely everything about you. It will have all of your information stored on it including bank account, medical records, social security number, driver's license, etc. Even further down the road, they will implant chips into our foreheads to interface with our brains to control thought signals. They will then record your every thought from birth to death and a computer will be able to analyze and predict all your behavior and know every thought you have.

So with all this technology in place, they will be able to have a one world government. It will not matter where you live, they can track you no matter where you are and know what you are doing, and who you are doing it with.

They will make you do work for free and will have large eating houses where you can go and scan in to get a bite to eat, but only enough to stay healthy enough to work, no more. You won't see any more of these fat kids running around either. That will all stop. They will need healthy slaves. In fact, in many workplaces today, you already see a trend toward this. There are lots of workplaces that have gyms built right into the office building where employees can stay fit and healthy.

What this all will lead to is a world where everyone works for free and will be happy about doing it. They will accomplish this by controlling your brain and thoughts through the computer chip in your head and causing you to really enjoy doing the work you have been programmed to do. You won't even want a paycheck, because they will make you believe that it's the right thing to do. They will make you serve all the way up until you die.

At a certain age, they will make the "logical" decision to "mortalize" you (kill you medically – probably with an injection) because you are no longer any value to society. They will just call your name up for the "retirement". You may receive a text message at a certain age that will contain your date and time of mortalization – you know, kind of like a social security report you get today. After all, you are only a product to keep their well oiled machine working. It works for them, but the question you must ask yourself is does it work for you?

Thank you for taking the time to read this information. I really enjoyed our time together even if it was just through some written words (could we consider it a long text?). Well, I hope that you will improve the quality of your life by getting closer to God and to nature. Spend time in the flesh with loved ones and lose all the electronic gadgets during your time spent with them. In fact, lose the clocks and watches. Try enjoying your life without these "limits" put on you by mankind for just a day here and there whenever you can and allow Jesus to set you free from all the slavery.